CW00434290

**Abound Academy**

Dedicated for your Abound success

# Microsoft Certified: PL 300 Power BI Data Analyst Associate Mock Tests

## 160+ Realistic Mock Tests to get you PL 300 certified on your 1st attempt

Abound Academy

Amazon Edition

This work is subject to copyright © 2024 Abound Academy. All rights are reserved by the Publisher, whether the whole or part of the material is concerned, specifically the rights of translation, reprinting, reuse of illustrations, recitation, broadcasting, reproduction on microfilms or in any other physical way, and transmission or information storage and retrieval, electronic adaptation, computer software, or by similar or dissimilar methodology now known or hereafter developed.

Trademarked names, logos, and images may appear in this book. Rather than use a trademark symbol with every occurrence of a trademarked name, logo, or image we use the names, logos, and images only in an editorial fashion and to the benefit of the trademark owner, with no intention of infringement of the trademark.

While the advice and information in this book are believed to be true and accurate at the date of publication, neither the authors nor the editors nor the publisher can accept any legal responsibility for any errors or omissions that may be made. The publisher makes no warranty, express or implied, with respect to the material contained herein.

**ISBN:** 9798842986668

**Imprint:** Independently published

For any other information, visit our website: www.aboundacademy.com, or contact our email helpdesk contact@aboundacademy.com.

The content of this book is aligned with the latest PL 300 Certification examination.
All rights reserved.

# About the Author

Abound Academy is a Professional Certification Provider Institution which provides content for major professional certification exams such as PMP®, Agile®, Disciplined Agile®, Scrum®, AWS®, Azure®, Python, PSM®, and many other such high-demand certifications. We offer our candidates with exam study materials like online courses, training books, realistic mock questions, and downloadable pdf for all the resources that are featured in our Academy. We help you to boost your professional career by providing a definitive way of getting you certified on your respective certification on your very 1st attempt.

As an academy, we have enabled more than 100,000 individuals with their certification requirements and delivered successful results for more than 50,000 students. Our mission is to act as a stimulant to bring a positive boost in career change for everyone. Our study material and exam simulators are made to help the professionals to get certified, and thus achieve their goals in their respective fields.

We believe that skills and their certification has the power to transform lives and the whole world. We are dedicated to providing best-in-industry training and mock tests that are delivered by highly experienced and competent industry experts. We thrive to work in partnership with communities over the boundaries. Our focus is to become the leading provider of high-quality online certification training to professionals over the boundaries.

Dedicated for your Abound success

# Preface

Are you looking for a comprehensive and reliable way to prepare for the PL 300 (DA-100) Power BI Data Analyst Associate exam? Do you want to test your skills and knowledge of Power BI and get ready to ace the exam on your first attempt? If yes, then this book is for you!

In today's fast-paced world, data is everywhere, and harnessing its power has become a crucial aspect of decision-making for businesses worldwide. Microsoft Power BI has emerged as a leading platform for data analysis and visualization, empowering organizations to derive valuable insights from their data to drive strategic initiatives. This book is designed to aid aspiring data professionals in their journey to become Microsoft Certified: Power BI Data Analyst Associates. Specifically tailored for the PL-300 exam, this comprehensive resource provides you with over **160 realistic mock tests**, meticulously crafted to simulate the exam experience and equip you with the knowledge and confidence needed to excel.

Throughout this book, you will encounter a diverse range of scenarios and questions, mirroring real-world challenges encountered by data analysts. By engaging with these mock tests, you will not only test your understanding of Power BI concepts but also refine your problem-solving skills and test-taking strategies, ultimately enhancing your readiness for the PL-300 exam.

By taking these mock tests, you will be able to:
- Assess your current level of proficiency and identify your strengths and weaknesses.
- Review the key concepts and skills required for the PL 300 exam, such as preparing, modeling, visualizing, analyzing, and deploying data with Power BI.
- Familiarize yourself with the exam structure, format, and question types.
- Gain confidence and reduce exam anxiety by practicing in a realistic environment.
- Learn from your mistakes and avoid common pitfalls and errors.
- Track your progress and measure your improvement over time.

This book is designed to help you achieve your goal of becoming a Microsoft Certified: Power BI Data Analyst Associate. Whether you are a beginner or an experienced Power BI user, this book will provide you with the essential tools and resources to prepare for the exam and boost your career. We understand the significance of obtaining industry-recognized certifications in today's competitive landscape. Therefore, our primary goal with this book is to provide you with a robust preparation resource that maximizes your chances of success on your first attempt at the PL-300 exam.

To get the most out of this book, we recommend that you:
- Review the exam objectives and study guide on the Microsoft Learn website.
- Watch the exam prep videos and demo the exam experience on the Microsoft Learn website.
- Take the mock tests in this book and review the explanations and references carefully.
- Repeat the mock tests until you achieve a consistent score of 80% or higher.

We extend our best wishes to you on your quest to become Microsoft Certified: Power BI Data Analyst Associates. May this book serve as a valuable tool in your pursuit of excellence, and may your efforts be rewarded with success.

Happy studying!

Abound Academy

# Table of Content

# Chapter 1: Introduction

Microsoft's PL-300 certification, also known as the Power BI Data Analyst certification, is designed for individuals who aim to deliver actionable insights by leveraging available data and applying domain expertise. This certification focuses on equipping professionals with the skills needed to work effectively with data and generate meaningful insights using Power BI, a powerful business analytics tool.

Data analysts leverage Microsoft Power BI to help businesses extract maximum value from their data assets. Serving as experts in their field, they undertake tasks such as designing and constructing scalable data models, refining and converting data, and implementing advanced analytical functions to generate easily understandable data visualizations that offer significant business insights. Furthermore, data analysts collaborate with various stakeholders across different sectors to provide pertinent insights aligned with specific business needs. It's essential for data analysts to possess a foundational understanding of data storage solutions and data processing methods, whether they are deployed on-premises or in the cloud.

## 1.1 Key Concepts Covered

1. **Power BI Overview:** Understanding the fundamentals of Power BI, including its features, capabilities, and functionalities.
2. **Data Analysis Techniques:** Learning various data analysis techniques to extract valuable insights from datasets.
3. **Data Visualization:** Mastering the art of data visualization to communicate insights effectively to stakeholders.
4. **Data Modeling:** Developing scalable data models to organize and structure data for analysis.
5. **Data Cleaning and Transformation:** Acquiring skills to clean and transform data for accurate analysis.
6. **Managing Workspaces:** Understanding how to manage workspaces within Power BI to collaborate and share insights with team members.

## 1.2 About the Exam

This exam is focused on skills in preparing, modeling, visualizing, and analyzing data to maximize value for an organization. Passing this exam will earn you the Microsoft Certified: Power BI Data Analyst Associate credential, which demonstrates your ability to deliver actionable insights by working with available data and applying domain expertise.

The following table summarizes the key details of the exam:

| Exam Name: | Microsoft Power BI Data Analyst (PL-300) |
|---|---|
| Certification: | Microsoft Certified: Power BI Data Analyst Associate |
| Exam Code: | PL-300 |
| Exam Duration: | 100 minutes (1 hour 40 minutes) |
| Exam Format: | Multiple-choice and multiple-select questions |
| No. of Questions: | 40-60 multiple-choice questions (including 1 case study) |
| Exam Cost: | $165 USD. |
| Languages Covered: | English, Japanese, Chinese (Simplified), Korean, German, French, Spanish, Portuguese (Brazil), Arabic (Saudi Arabia), Russian, Chinese (Traditional), Italian, Indonesian (Indonesia) |
| Prerequisites: | Basic understanding of data repositories and data processing (both on-premises and in the cloud) |
| Skills Measured: | This exam measures your ability to accomplish the following technical tasks: |

| | |
|---|---|
| | • Prepare the data (25–30%)<br>• Model the data (25–30%)<br>• Visualize and analyze the data (25–30%)<br>• Deploy and maintain items (15–20%) |

The PL-300 certificate is valid for 1 year. We have to renew this certificate within six months prior to its expiration date.

## 1.3 About the Candidates

As an aspiring candidate for the Microsoft Certified: PL-300 Power BI Data Analyst Associate certification, your goal is to provide actionable insights through the utilization of available data and the application of domain expertise. More specifically, you are expected to:

1. Provide meaningful business value through easy-to-comprehend data visualizations.
2. Enable others to perform self-service analytics.
3. Deploy and configure solutions for consumption.

As a Power BI data analyst, your role involves closely liaising with business stakeholders to discern their business needs. You collaborate with enterprise data analysts and data engineers to pinpoint and gather relevant data. Your expertise in utilizing Power BI encompasses:

• Transforming data.
• Creating data models.
• Visualizing data.
• Sharing assets.

Furthermore, it's important to have expertise in Power Query utilization and the ability to craft expressions with Data Analysis Expressions (DAX). A solid grasp of data quality evaluation and data security, encompassing aspects such as row-level security and data sensitivity, is indispensable.

## 1.4 Ten Practical Tips for a better Preparation

Preparing for the everchanging exam is a hassle. Trust us when it comes to the preparation part of it. Well, we have jotted down a few very simple and practical tips that will be highly effective for you for your PL 300 Exam preparation. Here are 10 practical and realistic tips to give you that extra edge to you to prepare effectively for the Microsoft Certified: PL-300 Power BI Data Analyst Associate exam:

**Tip 1. Understand the Exam Objectives:**
• Review the official exam objectives provided by Microsoft. Understand what skills and topics the exam covers. This will guide your study plan.

**Tip 2. Hands-On Practice with Power BI:**

- Use Power BI extensively. Create reports, dashboards, and visualizations. Practice data transformation, modeling, and DAX calculations.
- Explore sample datasets and build real-world scenarios.

**Tip 3. Learn Data Modeling Techniques:**
- Understand data modeling concepts such as relationships, hierarchies, and calculated columns.
- Practice creating efficient data models that optimize performance.

**Tip 4. Master DAX (Data Analysis Expressions):**
- DAX is crucial for creating custom calculations and measures in Power BI.
- Study DAX functions, syntax, and best practices.

**Tip 5. Explore Power Query (M):**
- Power Query is used for data transformation. Learn how to clean, shape, and load data from various sources.
- Practice merging tables, filtering data, and handling null values.

**Tip 6. Review Power BI Documentation:**
- Go through official Microsoft documentation for Power BI. Understand features, connectors, and visualization options.
- Explore Power BI community forums and blogs for practical tips and solutions.

**Tip 7. Take Practice Tests:**
- Use practice exams to assess your knowledge. Identify weak areas and focus on improving them. (*This is where this book will be effective*)
- Understand the question format and time management.

**Tip 8. Learn About Data Security and Row-Level Security:**
- Understand how to secure data in Power BI using roles and permissions.
- Explore row-level security to restrict data access based on user roles.

**Tip 9. Optimize Report Performance:**
- Learn techniques to improve report loading speed and responsiveness.
- Practice optimizing visuals, reducing data volume, and using incremental refresh.

**Tip 10. Simulate Real-World Scenarios:**
- Create mock business scenarios. Build end-to-end solutions using Power BI.
- Practice data exploration, storytelling, and sharing reports with stakeholders.
- Remember, consistent practice, hands-on experience, and a solid understanding of Power BI concepts will lead to success in the exam. Good luck!

# Chapter 2: Skills Measured

NOTE: The bullets that follow each of the skills measured are intended to illustrate how we are assessing that skill. This list is not definitive or exhaustive.

NOTE: Most questions cover features that are General Availability (GA). The exam may contain questions on Preview features if those features are commonly used.

NOTE: The below skills that are measured and their respective percentages are as of February 6, 2024. It is subject to **change periodically** to reflect skills that are required to perform a role.

## 2.1 Prepare the Data (25-30%)

### Get data from data sources

- Identify and connect to a data source
- Change data source settings, including credentials, privacy levels, and data source locations
- Select a shared semantic model, or create a local data model
- Choose between DirectQuery, Import, and Dual mode
- Change the value in a parameter

### Clean the data

- Evaluate data, including data statistics and column properties
- Resolve inconsistencies, unexpected or null values, and data quality issues
- Resolve data import errors

### Transform and load the data

- Select appropriate column data types
- Create and transform columns
- Transform a query
- Design a star schema that contains facts and dimensions
- Identify when to use reference or duplicate queries and the resulting impact
- Merge and append queries
- Identify and create appropriate keys for relationships
- Configure data loading for queries

## 2.2 Model the Data (25-30%)

### Design and implement a data model

- Configure table and column properties

- Implement role-playing dimensions
- Define a relationship's cardinality and cross-filter direction
- Create a common date table
- Implement row-level security roles

## Create model calculations by using DAX

- Create single aggregation measures
- Use CALCULATE to manipulate filters
- Implement time intelligence measures
- Identify implicit measures and replace with explicit measures
- Use basic statistical functions
- Create semi-additive measures
- Create a measure by using quick measures
- Create calculated tables

## Optimize model performance

- Improve performance by identifying and removing unnecessary rows and columns
- Improve performance by choosing optimal data types
- Identify poorly performing measures, relationships, and visuals by using Performance Analyzer
- Improve performance by summarizing data

# 2.3 Visualize and analyze the data (25-30%)

## Create reports

- Identify and implement appropriate visualizations
- Format and configure visualizations
- Use a custom visual
- Apply and customize a theme
- Configure conditional formatting
- Apply slicing and filtering
- Configure the report page
- Use the Analyze in Excel feature
- Choose when to use a paginated report

## Enhance reports for usability and storytelling

- Configure bookmarks
- Create custom tooltips
- Edit and configure interactions between visuals
- Configure navigation for a report
- Apply sorting

- Configure sync slicers
- Group and layer visuals by using the Selection pane
- Drill down into data using interactive visuals
- Configure export of report content, and perform an export
- Design reports for mobile devices

## Identify patterns and trends

- Use the Analyze feature in Power BI
- Use grouping, binning, and clustering
- Incorporate the Q&A feature in a report
- Use AI visuals
- Use reference lines, error bars, and forecasting
- Detect outliers and anomalies
- Create and share scorecards and metrics

# 2.4 Deploy and Maintain items (15-20%)

## Create and manage workspaces and items

- Create and configure a workspace
- Assign workspace roles
- Configure and update a workspace app
- Publish, import, or update items in a workspace
- Create dashboards
- Choose a distribution method
- Apply sensitivity labels to workspace content
- Configure subscriptions and data alerts
- Promote or certify Power BI content
- Manage global options for files

## Manage semantic models

- Identify when a gateway is required
- Configure a semantic model scheduled refresh
- Configure row-level security group membership
- Provide access to semantic models

# Chapter 3: PL 300 Mock Test 1

**Question 1:**
**CASE 1**
You are a Power BI specialist at your organization. In your finance table, you have a column called margin, which is defined as 'margin = revenue – cost of goods sold.' In your company, there are several different ways people refer to margin. Some people call margin by other terms such as income, profit or profit margin.
To use the Q&A feature successfully in your dashboard, you need to configure your dataset columns to enable users to type in variations for margin.
Solution: Add Synonyms to the finance table
Does this solution meet the goal?
    A. Yes
    B. No

**Question 2:**
**CASE 1**
You are a Power BI specialist at your organization. In your finance table, you have a column called margin, which is defined as 'margin = revenue – cost of goods sold.' In your company, there are several different ways people refer to margin. Some people call margin by other terms such as income, profit or profit margin.
To use the Q&A feature successfully in your dashboard, you need to configure your dataset columns to enable users to type in variations for margin.
Solution: Add a detailed description of how you defined margin
Does this solution meet the goal?
    A. Yes
    B. No

**Question 3:**
**CASE 1**
You are a Power BI specialist at your organization. In your inventory table, there are several different ways people refer to inventory. Some people call inventory by other terms such as stock, supply, parts or supply.
To use the Q&A feature successfully in your dashboard, you need to configure your inventory table and columns.
Solution: Set the row label on the inventory table
Does this solution meet the goal?
    A. Yes
    B. No

**Question 4:**
**CASE 1**
You are a Power BI specialist at your organization. In your inventory table, there are several different ways people refer to inventory. Some people call inventory by other terms such as stock, supply, parts or supply.
To use the Q&A feature successfully in your dashboard, you need to configure your inventory table and columns.
**Solution: Use Teach Q&A**
**Does this solution meet the goal?**
    A. Yes
    B. No


**Question 5:**
**CASE 2**
You have the below relationship between sales, product and employees. The employees table is joined to the product table by 'category', and the product table is joined to the sales table by 'ProductKey.'
Your boss asks you to build a visual for each Manager's sales by Subcategory.
What do you need to configure to solve that problem?

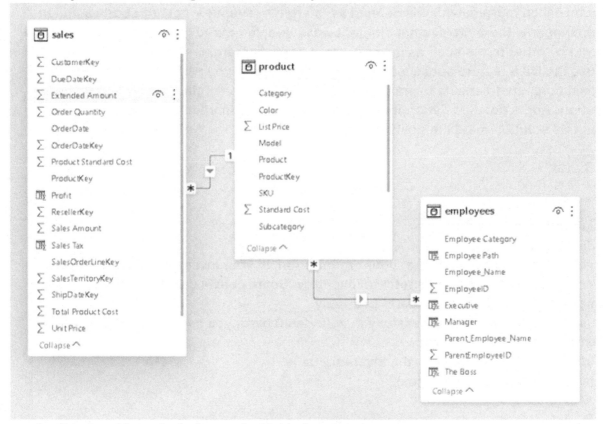

    A. Create a hierarchy in the product table for subcategory
    B. In the employees table, change Employee to type text
    C. Set the cross-filter between product and employees to both

D.  In the Model view, change the product table's toggle is hidden' to True

**Question 6:**
**CASE 2**
**You want to create a hierarchy in the products table for Category and Subcategory. You will then use the hierarchy as a drill down for a sales by product visualization as per the below exhibit. What three actions should you perform in sequence?**

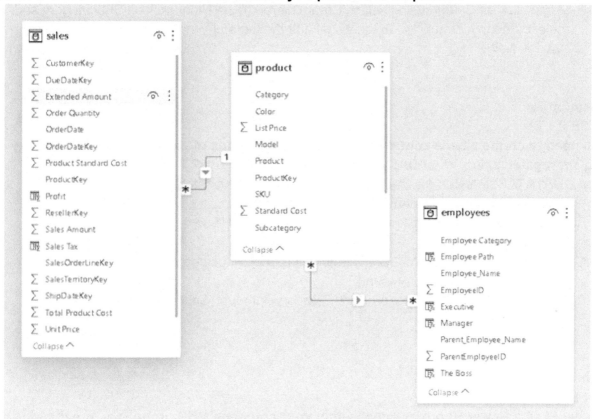

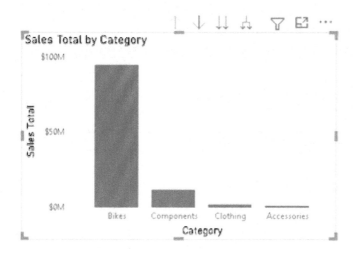

A. Right click on Category and select 'New Measure' -> Right click on Subcategory and select 'Add to hierarchy' -> In the visual add the hierarchy in the Axis and sales to the Values well

B. Right click on Category and select 'Create hierarchy' -> Add Subcategory to the drill through fields -> In the visual add the hierarchy in the Axis and sales to the Values well

C. Right click on Category and select 'Create hierarchy' -> Right click on Subcategory and select 'Add to hierarchy' -> In the visual add the category field to the Axis, which will automatically link the hierarchy

D. Right click on Category and select 'Create hierarchy' -> Right click on Subcategory and select 'Add to hierarchy' -> In the visual add the hierarchy in the Axis and sales to the Values well

## Question 7:
## CASE 2

**You need to create a table containing unique combinations of category and subcategory and aggregated sales. What DAX expression should you use?**

A. DATATABLE('sales','product' [Category], 'product' [Subcategory],"Sales Total",SUM(sales[Sales Amount]))

B. SUMMARIZECOLUMNS('product'[Category],'product'[Subcategory],sales[Sales Amount])

C. SUMMARIZE('sales','product' [Category],'product'[Subcategory],"Sales Total",SUM(sales[Sales Amount]))

D. SELECTCOLUMNS('sales,'product'[Category],'product'[Subcategory],sales[Sales Amount])

## Question 8:
## CASE 3

**You work as a Power BI professional within your company's HR group. You are creating a data model to use for reporting within the group. As you start building relationships, you see there are issues connecting some of the tables.**

**What two fixes are required to get the relationships working in your data model?**

| Table Name | Column Name | Data Type |
|---|---|---|
| Employees | EmployeeID | Whole number |
| | Hire Date | Date |
| | GenderID | Whole number |
| | AgeID | Whole number |
| | Ethnicity | Text |
| | Relocation | Text |
| | HR Manager | Text |

| Table Name | Column Name | Data Type |
|---|---|---|
| | Previous company | Text |
| | PayID | Percentage |
| | BUID | Whole number |
| PayType | PayID | Whole number |
| | Signing bonus | Fixed decimal |
| | Salary | Fixed decimal |
| AgeGroup | AgeID | Whole number |
| | AgeGroup | Text |
| BU | BUID | Text |
| | BU Name | Text |
| | Region | Text |
| Gender | GenderID | Whole number |
| | Gender | Text |

A. Change the data type of Employees[PayID] and hide Employees[Relocation] and Employees[HR Manager] fields
B. Change the data type of Employees[PayID] and BU[BUILD] to Whole Number
C. Ensure the cardinality between BU and Employees from Many to one (*:1) to Many to many (*:*)
D. Change the data type of Employees[PayID] and BU[BUILD] to Text

**Question 9:**
**CASE 3**
**You work as a Power BI professional within your company's HR group. The report you created for retention analysis worked fine in the development environment, but when deployed has performance issues.**
**Solution: Remove columns from the data model not used in reports**
**Does this solution meet the goal?**

| Table Name | Column Name | Data Type |
|---|---|---|
| Employees | EmployeeID | Whole number |
| | Hire Date | Date |
| | GenderID | Whole number |
| | AgeID | Whole number |
| | Ethnicity | Text |
| | Relocation | Text |
| | HR Manager | Text |
| | Previous company | Text |

| Table Name | Column Name | Data Type |
|---|---|---|
| | PayID | Percentage |
| | BUID | Whole number |
| PayType | PayID | Whole number |
| | Signing bonus | Fixed decimal |
| | Salary | Fixed decimal |
| AgeGroup | AgeID | Whole number |
| | AgeGroup | Text |
| BU | BUID | Text |
| | BU Name | Text |
| | Region | Text |
| Gender | GenderID | Whole number |
| | Gender | Text |

    A. Yes

    B. No.


**Question 10:**

**CASE 3**

You work as a Power BI professional within your company's HR group. The report you created for retention analysis worked fine in the development environment, but when deployed has performance issues.

Solution: Hide columns and tables from the data model not used in reports

Does this solution meet the goal?

| Table Name | Column Name | Data Type |
|---|---|---|
| Employees | EmployeeID | Whole number |
| | Hire Date | Date |
| | GenderID | Whole number |
| | AgeID | Whole number |
| | Ethnicity | Text |
| | Relocation | Text |
| | HR Manager | Text |
| | Previous company | Text |
| | PayID | Percentage |
| | BUID | Whole number |

22

| PayType | PayID | Whole number |
|---------|-------|--------------|
|  | Signing bonus | Fixed decimal |
|  | Salary | Fixed decimal |
| AgeGroup | AgeID | Whole number |
|  | AgeGroup | Text |
| BU | BUID | Text |
|  | BU Name | Text |
|  | Region | Text |
| Gender | GenderID | Whole number |
|  | Gender | Text |

A. Yes

B. No.

## Question 11:

You find an interesting visualization using the Python programming language that you want to run in Power BI. What are the three steps required before you can use Python in Power BI?

A. Install Python on your local machine

B. Enable R scripting

C. Install the libraries matplotlib and pandas

D. Enable Python scripting

E. Install the libraries seaborn and keras

## Question 12:

You are asked to optimize the performance of your data model. You have several intermediate queries that are not used for visualization and you have a large transactional table with a Date/Time field. What two optimizations should you do?

A. Change all relationship cross filter directions to single

B. Split the Date/Time field into a separate Date column and a separate Time column

C. Turn off single select on slicers

D. Disable Power Query load on intermediary queries

## Question 13:

You receive a new table to incorporate into your analysis in Power BI. You use Power Query to preview the data. For each of the following statements, select Yes if the statement is true. Otherwise, select No.

| Statement | Yes | No |
|---|---|---|
| By default, Data Preview analyzes the first 5,000 rows in the dataset. | | |
| When you hover your mouse over column quality, you can see both number and percentage of valid, error and empty cells. | | |
| You can use the entire dataset for column profiling. | | |

A. Yes / Yes / Yes
B. No / Yes / Yes
C. No / Yes / No
D. No / No / Yes


## Question 14:

You are the Power BI administrator at your company which builds VR headsets. You need to assign appropriate workspace roles to your colleagues and must use the lowest permission necessary to accomplish the task. Which roles should you use for the below workspace requirements?
1. **Update and delete workspaces**
2. **Publish apps**
3. **Publish content to the workspace**

A. Member / Member / Contributor
B. Member! Member/Viewer
C. Admin / Member/ Contributor
D. Admin / Admin / Contributor


## Question 15:

You have a table of temperatures for various cities. Some cities use Fahrenheit, while others use Celsius. You need to write a DAX expression to create a new column called Category for the following conditions.
· If the value is greater than 80 and Units are F, then 'Hot'. Otherwise 'Not Hot'
· If the value is greater than 26 and Units are C, then 'Hot'. Otherwise 'Not Hot'
Complete the below DAX expression by replacing [VALUE]:
Category =
[VALUE] ( [VALUE] ( [VALUE] (Temperature[Value] > 80,Temperature[Units]="F"),
[VALUE] (Temperature[Value] > 26,Temperature[Units]="C") ),"Hot","Not Hot")

| City | Value | Units |
|------|-------|-------|
| Austin | 90 | F |
| Baltimore | 79 | F |
| Boise | 76 | F |
| Calgary | 20 | C |
| Chicago | 72 | F |
| Detroit | 70 | F |
| Houston | 97 | F |
| Montréal | 27 | C |
| Nashville | 78 | F |
| Ottawa | 24 | C |

A. SWITCH/ AND / OR / AND
B. SWITCH /OR / OR / AND
C. IF / OR / AND / AND
D. IF / AND / OR / AND
E. WHILE / AND / OR / AND


**Question 16:**

**Your boss has scrolled through the Theme Gallery on the website https://community.powerbi.com/.**
**She asks you to use a particular theme for your company's report in Power BI Service. How do you incorporate the theme in your report?**

A. Download the JSON file and in Custom Dashboard theme > Upload JSON theme
B. Download the CSS file and in Custom Dashboard theme > Upload CSS theme
C. Download the PNG file and right-click on a tile > Upload PNG theme
D. Download the PDF file and right-click on the dashboard > Upload PDF theme


**Question 17:**

**You are your company's Power BI expert. You know that data lineage shows you which data sources are used by which datasets. One of your colleagues says he cannot access data lineage. What could be two possible explanations for data lineage not working?**

A. Only admins can see the lineage view
B. You need a Power BI Pro license to see lineage view
C. Lineage only works for DirectQuery datasets
D. Lineage view is available only to users with higher than Viewer access to the workspace
E. Each user needs to be granted lineage view permission in the tenant settings

**Question 18:**
You have a data set that shows employees and their bosses, as per the exhibit below. There is a field for each Employee called Employee_Name and a field for their boss Parent_Employee_Name. How would you create the Employee_Hierarchy column with a delimited hierarchy list in DAX?

| EmployeeID | Employee_Name | Parent_EmployeeID | Parent_Employee_Name | Employee_Hierarchy |
|---|---|---|---|---|
| 111 | Steven May | | | Steven May |
| 2 | Nathan Jones | 111 | Steven May | Steven May \| Nathan Jones |
| 3 | Christian Salem | 2 | Nathan Jones | Steven May \| Nathan Jones \| Christian Salem |
| 4 | James Harmes | 3 | Christian Salem | Steven May \| Nathan Jones \| Christian Salem \| James Harmes |
| 5 | Chris Petracca | 3 | Christian Salem | Steven May \| Nathan Jones \| Christian Salem \| Chris Petracca |

A. PATHITEM(employees[Employee_Name], employees[Parent_Employee_Name])
B. RELATED(employees[Parent_Employee_Name], employees[Employee_Name])
C. CONCATENATE(employees[Parent_Employee_Name], employees[Employee_Name])
D. PATH(employees[Employee_Name], employees[Parent_Employee_Name])


**Question 19:**
You work for a computer accessories company and your data model contains the following tables:
1. Accessories table: 1k rows that are updated monthly
2. Sales table: 15M rows that are updated regularly with changes that need to be shown immediately
3. Date table: 10k rows that are updated rarely
For the three tables ABOVE, which storage mode should you use from the below options?
- Import
- DirectQuery
- Dual

A. Accessories: Import / Sales: DirectQuery/ Date: Dual
B. Accessories: Import / Sales: DirectQuery/ Date: Import
C. Accessories: DirectQuery / Sales: Import I Date: DirectQuery


**Question 20:**
You work for a consulting company that has a contract with a large government department. Part of the requirements for the report is to configure the page for use with a screen reader for sight-impaired users. What should you configure in your report such that the page follows a logical sequence?
A. Bookmarks

B. Tab order
C. Filters on all pages
D. Layer order

**Question 21:**

**You work at a sports betting company and have a table with US soccer scores and a second table with betting odds. Both tables share a common key called GameID. Your boss asks you to create a new combined table. Which transform should you use to create the dataset?**

A. Append queries as new
B. Append queries
C. Merge queries as new
D. Merge queries

**Question 22:**

**You work for a transportation company that uses Azure IoT devices to monitor the temperature within containers. The head of Supply Chain has asked you to create a dashboard for the streaming data from the IoT devices and you need to configure Power BI appropriately. For each of the following statements, select Yes if the statement is true. Otherwise, select No.**

| Statement | Yes | No |
|---|---|---|
| You can build report visuals using the data that flows in from the stream. | | |
| Visualize a streaming dataset by adding a dashboard tile. | | |
| Streaming data can make use of report functionality such as filtering. | | |

A. No / Yes / No
B. Yes / Yes / No
C. No / No / Yes
D. No / No / No

**Question 23:**

**You are part of a planning team and are investigating the forecast accuracy across multiple plants, various products and a series of demand types (e.g. stable, seasonal, growing etc.) You use Power BI and know that there is a visual that can help you with the root cause of low forecast accuracy. Which visual should you choose?**

A. Waterfall
B. Treemap
C. Key influencers
D. Decomposition tree


**Question 24:**
**You work for a baseball hat retailer and you need to create a table of the top 3 team names by the total number of transactions. You have a table called Hat Sales and another for Team. Select the proper DAX functions to correctly complete the formula by replacing the [VALUE] field:**
**Top Hat Sales = [VALUE] ( 3,**
**[VALUE] ( HatSales, HatTeams[Team Name], "Transactions",**
**COUNT(HatSales[TransactionID])**
**), [Transactions],DESC)**

| Table Name | Column Name |
|------------|-------------|
| Hat Sales | TransactionID |
| | Date |
| | TeamID |
| | Units |
| | Amount |
| Team | TeamID |
| | Team Name |
| | Team Location |

A. RANKX - CALCULATE
B. TOPN - CALCULATE
C. FILTER - SUMMARIZE
D. TOPN - SUMMARIZE


**Question 25:**
**You import a large table from Excel into Power BI and you suspect there may be missing data. How would you find the percentage of empty cells in each column?**
A. Column quality
B. Column profile
C. Show whitespace
D. Column distribution

**Question 26:**

You work for a shoe distribution company and your firm uses Power BI for reporting. One of the reports you have created is exported as a PDF so the warehouse staff can check off items on a hard copy. Your company, however, has a policy that all exported reports need to be encrypted. How can you meet this requirement?

    A. Use Row Level Security (RLS)
    B. Set the PDF options in the tenant settings
    C. Configure the dataset build permission security options
    D. Use sensitivity labels

**Question 27:**

You work for a share trading software company and have a dashboard for user trading times. The data set used for the analysis goes back seven years. When the data reloads, it takes excessive time as the full seven years are refreshed. How can you improve the dataset performance?

    A. Use an on-premises data gateway
    B. Configure incremental refresh in Power BI Desktop and enable it in Power BI service
    C. Enable incremental refresh directly in Power BI service
    D. Manually refresh the database when users are not active

**Question 28:**

You are in Power Query Editor and you see the below highlighted in the red box. What data preview option is used to create these charts?

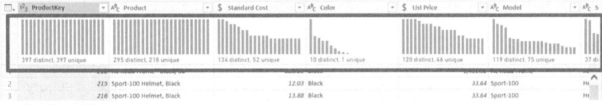

    A. Monospace
    B. Column distribution
    C. Column quality
    D. Column profile

**Question 29:**

You have a data model with two key tables: Region and Shipping. There is a one-to-many relationship between the Region and the Shipping table. The model also has two row-level security roles named Region_Texas and Shipping_Mode The DAX filters for the two security roles are:

    • **Region_Texas filter is: Region[state] = "Texas"**

- **Shipping_Mode filter is: Shipping[mode] = "Rail"**

**If a manager is a member of both the Region_Texas and Shipping_Mode roles, what will they see in a report using this data model?**

    A. The user will only see data for the state of Texas.
    B. The user will only see data for the rail shipping mode.
    C. The user will see data for which the state is Texas AND the shipping model is rail.
    D. The user will see data for which the state is Texas OR the shipping mode is rail.

**Question 30:**
**You create an R visual in Power BI that has 500,000 rows. You notice that not all the data is shown and a message is displayed on the image. Your boss asks you the cause of this issue. What is the reason not all data is shown?**

    A. You are using a version prior to 2.0 of the plotly library
    B. You are missing an R package
    C. The visual has too many rows
    D. The resolution is too high

**Question 31:**
**You have one report page with multiple visuals that is running slow, leading to complaints from users. What TWO solutions will help optimize your visuals?**

    A. Don't use multiple colors on bar charts
    B. Apply filters to reduce the max number of items that a visual displays
    C. Replace the default visuals with custom visuals
    D. Limit the use of bar charts
    E. Limit the number of visuals on a particular report page to only what is necessary

**Question 32:**
**You are asked to create a category percentage measure that will reflect the values selected when using a slicer. In the output below, you will see that the Bikes category is not selected in the slicer and the category percentage reflects the current filter context. All category percentage values add to 100% of the filter context. You are given a measure that sums the sales called Sales Total. How would you create a category percentage measure in DAX?**

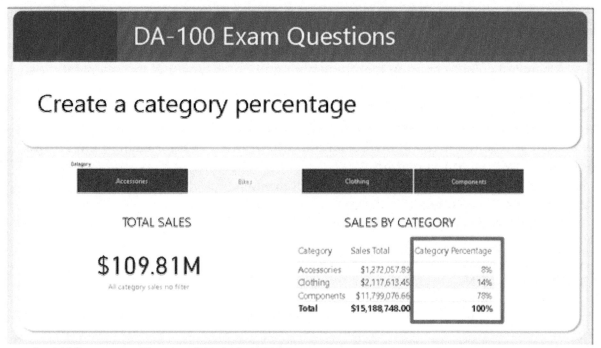

A. VAR categoryTotal = CALCULATE([Sales Total],ALL('product' [Category])) VAR categoryPercentage = DIVIDE([Sales Total],categoryTotal) RETURN categoryPercentage

B. VAR categoryTotal = [Sales Total] VAR categoryPercentage = DIVIDE([Sales Total],categoryTotal) RETURN categoryPercentage

C. VAR categoryTotal = CALCULATE([Sales Total],ALLSELECTED('product'[Category])) VAR categoryPercentage = DIVIDE([Sales Total], categoryTotaL) RETURN categoryPercentage

D. VAR categoryTotal = CALCULATE([Sales Total],REMOVEFILTERS('product'[Category])) VAR categoryPercentage = DIVIDE([Sales Total],categoryTotal) RETURN categoryPercentage

**Question 33:**
**You work for a Japanese auto company whose fiscal year starts April 1. You have a table called Cars with orders for cars. You need to create a common date for a data model using DAX, respecting the fiscal period. How should you create a date table using DAX?**

A. CALENDAR(4)

B. CALENDAR( DATE (20O031), DATE (YEAR (LASTDATE (Cars[OrderDate] )), 31, 3

C. CALENDAR( DATE (YEAR ( FIRSTDATE ( Cars[OrderDate] ),4,1), DATE ( 2025, 12, 31 ))

D. CALENDARAUTO(3)

**Question 34:**
**You work in the spare parts department of an oil and gas company as a BI expert. The company has hundreds of parts, ten years of historic data, and hundreds of different**

order sizes from suppliers. You create a report in Power BI with aggregations for the following visuals:
- A column chart of parts on the axis, but there are too many products showing
- A stacked column chart of month number and order type, but too many months show
- A histogram of supplier order sizes, but there are too many order sizes

You need to combine the data to make the visual more readable.

How should you combine the data? Select the GROUPING TYPE for each of the THREE solutions below from top to bottom.

1. Combined the product into categories of product
2. Combine the columns into 3 month number blocks
3. Combine order sizes into 8 groups

A. LIST / BIN / LIST
B. LIST / BIN / BIN
C. BIN / LIST / LIST
D. BIN / LIST / BIN


Question 35:
You are analyzing basketball total points for the NBA for the year 2021. You have a measure [Points Total] which sums up the points and a date table with a year column. How should you complete the below DAX formula to effectively use it independently from any other filters set on the report page? Select the appropriate DAX function in place of [VALUE].
Sales 2021 =
CALCULATE(
[Points Total],
FILTER( [VALUE] ('Date'[Year]), 'Date'[Year] = 2021)
)

A. PATH
B. ALL
C. ALLEXCEPT
D. RELATED


Question 36:
You want to use insights in Power BI Desktop to understand the increase from one quarter to the next in your sales column chart. Normally you would right-click the appropriate column and click on Analyze > Explain increase. However, this time insights does not appear to be available.

What are TWO possible reasons insights are not working?

A. You use hierarchies
B. You use TOPN filters

C.  You have filtered measures
D.  You use a stacked column chart

## Question 37:
You work for an aerospace company in their satellite division. You build a workspace called 'satellite apps' in Power BI service that contains several reports and management level apps. You have a new analyst come on board and need to allow them to edit and publish reports. How would you achieve this goal?
A.  Configure the security group from Azure Active Directory
B.  Add the user as a member in the role section of the 'satellite apps' workspace
C.  In Power BI Desktop set Row Level Security (RLS)
D.  Within the 'satellite apps' workspace, select update app

## Question 38:
You have a line chart that shows units manufactured by month. You want to add the on-time delivery metric for each month when you hover the mouse over a data point. How would you provide the additional piece of data?
A.  Add on-time delivery to the drillthrough fields
B.  Add the on-time delivery column to the secondary values field
C.  Add on-time delivery column to the tooltips field
D.  Add the on-time delivery column to the small multiples field

## Question 39:
You create a Power BI report with a line chart as per the below exhibit. How do you add the dotted horizontal line for the mean values?

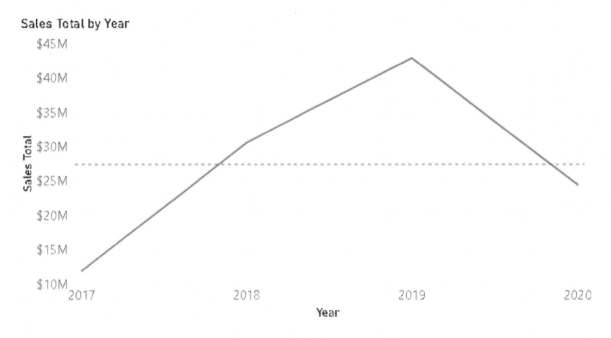

Sales Total by Year

A. Add a fixed forecast line for the time series in the analytics pane
B. Add an Average line for Sales Total in the analytics pane
C. Add a trend line across years in the analytics pane
D. Add a min line in the analytics pane

**Question 40:**
**You have built several DAX measures. A senior Power BI member of your team asks you to improve the performance and readability of the below DAX expression? How would you achieve this goal?**
**Annual Sales Growth % =**
**DIVIDE(**
**([Sales] - CALCULATE([Sales], PARALLELPERIOD('Date'[Date], -12, MONTH))),**
**CALCULATE([Sales], PARALLELPERIOD('Date'[Date], -12, MONTH))**
**)**

A. Replace DIVIDE with a simple divide calculation using the '/' symbol
B. Instead of PARALLELPERIOD(), use DATEADD()
C. Mark date table as date
D. Use VARIABLES and a RETURN statement

**Question 41:**
**You work for a forklift manufacturer. You are building a data model in Power BI and have a sales table as per the below exhibit. Within the sales table, there is a field called Model. How would you complete the DAX expression below to generate a Model table? What would you fill in for the [VALUE] fields starting from left to right?**
**Model Table = [VALUE] ( [VALUE] )**

| Table Name | Column Name |
|---|---|
| Sales | TransactionID |
| | Date |
| | Category |
| | Subcategory |
| | Model |
| | Model Desc |
| | Units |
| | Amount |

    A. CALCULATE / Sales[Model]
    B. DISTINCT / Sales[Model]
    C. CALCULATE / (Sales[Model] Model = "XPR")
    D. DISTINCT / Sales[Model Desc]

**Question 42:**
**You work for an eCommerce company that sells ergonomic office products. You are tasked with creating a Power BI report from your company's transactional sales data in a table called 'ergoSales'. Before you do anything with the data, you want to check that there are no negative amounts in the 'ergoSales'[quantity] field.**
**What is the most efficient way to check your data for negatives before creating the data model?**
    A. Select Column profile and then click on 'ergoSales'[quantity]
    B. Select Column quality and then click on ergoSales'[quantity]
    C. Click on 'ergoSales'[quantity] and select replace values
    D. Create a custom column using a conditional statement to filter negatives out

**Question 43:**
**You work for a diesel engine company as an internal Power BI consultant. You have two tables as per the below exhibit. There are no unique values in either table. However, the tables are related by Model Name.**
**You need to create relationships in the data model to enable a visual containing data from both tables.**
**How would you model these two tables in the most efficient manner?**

| Table Name | Column Name |
|---|---|
| ConnectingRod | RodID |
| | Manufacture Date |
| | Supplier Name |
| | Model Name |
| CyclinderHead | CylinderID |
| | Manufacture Date |
| | Factory Name |
| | Model Name |

A. Set the relationship between the two tables as one-to-one
B. Set the relationship between the two tables as many-to-many
C. Create a bridging table using unique IDs and create two one-to-many relationships
D. Set the relationship between the two tables as one-to-many

**Question 44:**

**You work for a manufacturing company with a metric called Supplied in Full on Time (SIFOT). In Power BI, you have built a dashboard to help management keep track of key summary data and metrics. One of your visuals is a gauge chart that shows the SIFOT values. The management team wants a notification to be sent when SIFOT drops below 85%. You need to configure email alerts to management when this happens. Which four actions should you perform to create this alert?**

A. Select + Add alert rule, ensure the Active slider is set to On
B. In the alert conditions choose 'below' and enter in a value of 85
C. Choose More options on the SIFOT gauge visual and select Manage alerts
D. In the dropdown for notification type, select email
E. In the alert conditions choose 'below' and enter in a value of 0.85
F. Check the 'Send me email too' and then save and close

**Question 45:**

**You are the head of analytics for a software company, and you want to understand the importance of factors that drive sales in your pre-sales team. What visual in Power BI can help you achieve your goal?**

A. Custom R Dumbell Plot

B. Q&A
C. Decomposition Tree
D. Key Influencers


**Question 46:**
You are editing the 'Model' column in a 'product' table Power Query. You need to replace instances of 'LL Road Frame' with 'JJ Roadster' and the previous step is 'Changed Type.' What M code functions would you use for the two [VALUE] fields?
= Table. [VALUE] (#"Changed Type","LL Road Frame","JJ
Roadster",Replacer. [VALUE],{"Model"})

A. ReplaceValue / ReplaceText
B. Replace Rows / ReplaceText
C. ReplaceText / ReplaceValue
D. ReplaceRows / ReplaceValue


**Question 47:**
You work in the marketing division for a sports apparel company. You have a sales fact table and multiple dimension tables as per the below exhibit. The head of marketing wants to encourage self-service analytics within the company and asks that you set up Q&A in the reports. Which of the following configurations will allow Q&A to work in your data model?

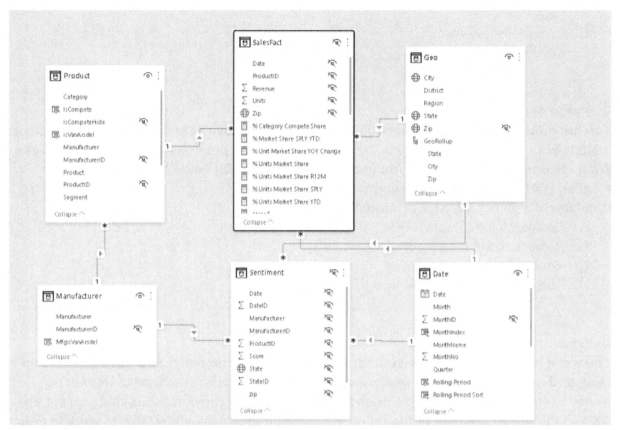

A. Object level security with any type of data source
B. Import
C. Composite models
D. Reporting Services

**Question 48:**
**You have sales data by day in a time series chart and need to produce a 25 day forecast with a 90% confidence interval as per the below exhibit. There are some data anomalies in the last 5 days of data that you want to ignore for the forecast. Select the THREE actions required to create the forecast.**

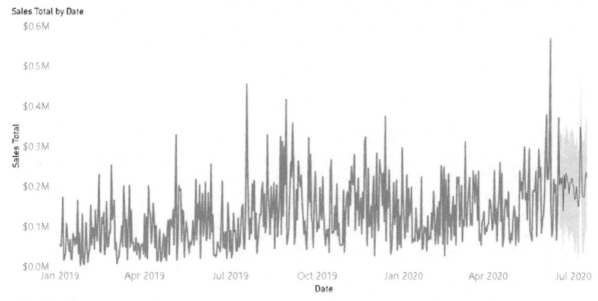

A. Set forecast length to 25 months and ignore last 5 months
B. Go to the analytics pane and under forecast select '+ Add'
C. Set the seasonality interval to 90% and click on apply
D. Set forecast length to 25 points and ignore last 5 points
E. Set the confidence interval to 90% and click on apply
F. Go to the analytics pane and under forecast select 'Add new trend'

**Question 49:**
You have a busy report page called Sales and decide to use a detailed chart in a separate page using the drill through feature. The Sales page shows a visual of total sales by month. When you click on drill through on the sales by month chart, it should redirect to a detail page called Sales Detail that shows sales for the selected month by category. The Sales Detail page should also preserve the filters from the original sales page. What FOUR actions should you perform?
A. On the Sales Detail page, under drill through option add month as the drill through field
B. On the Sales page, under drill through option add month as the drill through field
C. Create a new page called Sales Detail
D. On the Sales Detail page under Drill through, toggle Keep all filters on
E. Create a table visual to show total sales by month and category
F. On the Sales page under Drill through, toggle Keep all filters on

**Question 50:**
You are asked to present your findings on your company's warehousing performance across several years. You have a number of column and line charts and a date slicer. You decide you will create a presentation using Power BI and will create a narrative using the date slicer. What should you do to save the views across different years for your presentation?

A. Create page level filters and create a new groups
B. Filter the charts using the date slicer, then create bookmarks
C. Create drill throughs for each of the warehouse charts
D. Create report level filters and create a new groups

## Question 51:

You work in a marketing department as a Power BI professional. You are asked to create three different types of visuals for the marketing department. Which visualization should you use for the below three requirements?

1. Show progress of conversion rates against a target
2. Identify outliers in sentiment scores
3. Show the factors that influence sentiment scores

A. KPI / Waterfall / Treemap
B. Card / Scatter / Funnel
C. KPI / Scatter / Key influencers
D. Card / Funnel / Scatter

## Question 52:

You have built a report with multiple visuals for your food manufacturing company. As many senior members are often on the road, they ask that the reports be available for mobile devices. You need to optimize the report for mobile devices for the most critical visuals. Which three things can you do to optimize reports for mobile?

A. Set slicers to be responsive
B. Add the most important visuals to the mobile canvas
C. Set the page size as tablet or smartphone
D. Resize the visuals to fit the mobile canvas
E. Add haptic feedback (vibration) for when a user taps a visual
F. Remove chart axes

## Question 53:

You work for a College Football team as a Power BI sports analyst. You have built a report in Power BI Desktop that contains many visuals. The coaching team is pleased with the content of the visuals but wants the colors to match the college's color style guide. What should you do?

A. Adjust the report CSS file
B. Customize the current theme
C. Change the fonts on each text box
D. Change the colors on each visual

## Question 54:

You work for a microbrewery as head of data visualization. You have a Power BI data model that relies on several Excel files that reside on your company's internal server. You are emailed a new Excel workbook from the CEO that contains updated data. You place the new Excel workbook on your server and append the text 'v1.2' to the name. For each of the following statements, select Yes if the statement is true. Otherwise, select No.

| Statement | Yes | No |
|---|---|---|
| The new Excel file must have the same structure as the original workbook. | | |
| The new Excel workbook will only work if it has the exact same name and path as the previous file. | | |
| You can refresh the local Excel file by pressing F5 in Power BI. | | |

A. Yes / No / No
B. Yes / No / Yes
C. No / Yes / Yes
D. No / Yes / No


## Question 55:
Your company uses Power BI Premium and your manager wants to create printed invoices. However, the reports must fit perfectly on a page. What would you suggest to your manager?
A. Change the page view in Power BI Desktop
B. Use paginated reports
C. Use gridlines and snap to grid
D. Use lock objects


## Question 56:
You work in a shoe company's reporting team and have been tasked with building a Power BI report showing procurement analytics. You have an on-premises Microsoft SQL Server database that you use to build the procurement report using a DirectQuery connection. You thoroughly test the report and then upload it to Power BI Service. However, once in Power BI Service, the visualizations no longer work. How would you solve this problem?
A. Change the permissions on your Microsoft SQL Server database
B. Upgrade your Power BI Desktop
C. Install an on-premise data gateway
D. Install Power BI Report Builder

# 3.1 Mock Test 1 Answer Sheet

**Question 1:**
**CASE 1**
**You are a Power BI specialist at your organization. In your finance table, you have a column called margin, which is defined as 'margin = revenue – cost of goods sold.' In your company, there are several different ways people refer to margin. Some people call margin by other terms such as income, profit or profit margin.**
**To use the Q&A feature successfully in your dashboard, you need to configure your dataset columns to enable users to type in variations for margin.**
**Solution: Add Synonyms to the finance table**
**Does this solution meet the goal?**
  A. Yes
  B. No

**Answer: A.**

Explanation
The answer is A.
In the modeling tab in Power BI Desktop, you can add synonyms to a column. When a user uses Q&A, Power BI will check for synonyms when interpreting the question.

**Question 2:**
**CASE 1**
**You are a Power BI specialist at your organization. In your finance table, you have a column called margin, which is defined as 'margin = revenue – cost of goods sold.' In your company, there are several different ways people refer to margin. Some people call margin by other terms such as income, profit or profit margin.**
**To use the Q&A feature successfully in your dashboard, you need to configure your dataset columns to enable users to type in variations for margin.**
**Solution: Add a detailed description of how you defined margin**
**Does this solution meet the goal?**
  A. Yes
  B. No

**Answer: B.**

Explanation
The answer is B.
In the modeling section, you can add a description within the properties of a column. A description is helpful for other modelers to understand the purpose of the column. However, this description does not have any impact on how Q&A interprets synonyms.

**Question 3:**
**CASE 1**
**You are a Power BI specialist at your organization. In your inventory table, there are several different ways people refer to inventory. Some people call inventory by other terms such as stock, supply, parts or supply.**
**To use the Q&A feature successfully in your dashboard, you need to configure your inventory table and columns.**
**Solution: Set the row label on the inventory table**
**Does this solution meet the goal?**
   A.  Yes
   B.  No

**Answer: A.**

Explanation
The answer is A.
When you click on the table name in the modeling view, you can assign a row label to the column. A role label allows you to define which column best identifies a row in the table. This label assists Q&A to generate better visualizations as it knows the best column that identifies a table.

**Question 4:**
**CASE 1**
**You are a Power BI specialist at your organization. In your inventory table, there are several different ways people refer to inventory. Some people call inventory by other terms such as stock, supply, parts or supply.**
**To use the Q&A feature successfully in your dashboard, you need to configure your inventory table and columns.**
**Solution: Use Teach Q&A**
**Does this solution meet the goal?**
   A.  Yes
   B.  No

**Answer: A.**

Explanation
The answer is A.
When you click on the Q&A setup button in the home ribbon on Power BI Desktop, one of the options is to Teach Q&A. Teach Q&A allows you to enter a question in the language that someone in your organization may use such as 'What was my stock at the end of August.' If Power BI does not understand a word such as 'stock', you are prompted to define what 'stock' refers to. This way, when someone asks a similar question, Power BI will interpret the question correctly.

**Question 5:**
**CASE 2**
You have the below relationship between sales, product and employees. The employees table is joined to the product table by 'category', and the product table is joined to the sales table by 'ProductKey.'
Your boss asks you to build a visual for each Manager's sales by Subcategory.
What do you need to configure to solve that problem?

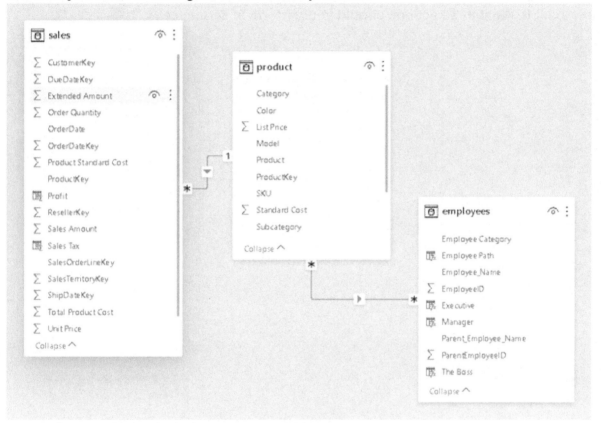

A. Create a hierarchy in the product table for subcategory
B. In the employees table, change Employee to type text
C. Set the cross-filter between product and employees to both
D. In the Model view, change the product table's toggle is hidden' to True

**Answer: C.**

Explanation
The answer is C.
The current filter direction on the employees table does not allow you to select manager and the sales and category fields. You need to alter the cross-filter direction to enable the filter to flow from the employees table to the product table.
Creating a hierarchy in the product table does not help with the cross-filter direction issue in the employees table.
Changing the EmployeeID to type text is not relevant. The key used to join the employees and product tables is 'category.' Toggling the product's table to hidden will prevent users from

seeing the product table. We want to use the fields in the products table to create visuals. This will not help solve our issue.

**Question 6:**
**CASE 2**
**You want to create a hierarchy in the products table for Category and Subcategory. You will then use the hierarchy as a drill down for a sales by product visualization as per the below exhibit. What three actions should you perform in sequence?**

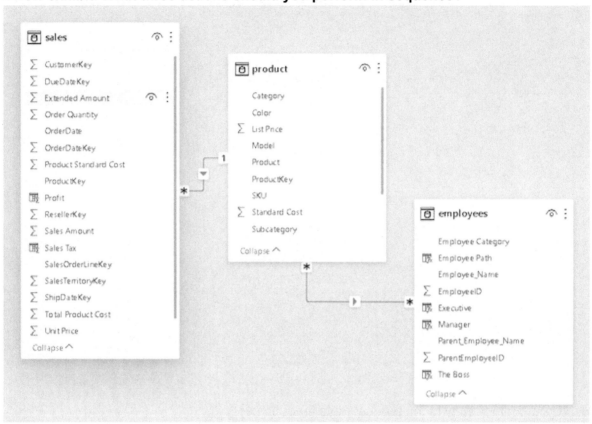

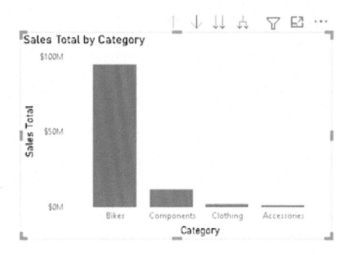

A. Right click on Category and select 'New Measure' -> Right click on Subcategory and select 'Add to hierarchy' -> In the visual add the hierarchy in the Axis and sales to the Values well

B. Right click on Category and select 'Create hierarchy' -> Add Subcategory to the drill through fields -> In the visual add the hierarchy in the Axis and sales to the Values well

C. Right click on Category and select 'Create hierarchy' -> Right click on Subcategory and select 'Add to hierarchy' -> In the visual add the category field to the Axis, which will automatically link the hierarchy

D. Right click on Category and select 'Create hierarchy' -> Right click on Subcategory and select 'Add to hierarchy' -> In the visual add the hierarchy in the Axis and sales to the Values well

**Answer: D.**

Explanation
The answer is D.
The set of steps to create a hierarchy and the drill down visual are:
1. Right click on Category and select 'Create hierarchy'
2. Right click on Subcategory and select 'Add to hierarchy'
3. In the visual add the hierarchy in the Axis and sales to the Values well

In answer A, you should not click on 'New Measure'. You want to create a hierarchy and not a measure.

In answer B, you should not add Subcategory to drill through. Subcategory needs to be added to the hierarchy. A drill through is used to create a page in your report that focuses on a specific entity.

In answer C, adding the category field to the Axis of your visual will not automatically link to the new hierarchy you have created. You need to add the hierarchy to the Axis field and sales to the Values field.

**Question 7:**
**CASE 2**
**You need to create a table containing unique combinations of category and subcategory and aggregated sales. What DAX expression should you use?**
A. DATATABLE('sales','product' [Category], 'product' [Subcategory],"Sales Total",SUM(sales[Sales Amount]))
B. SUMMARIZECOLUMNS('product'[Category],'product'[Subcategory],sales[Sales Amount])
C. SUMMARIZE('sales','product' [Category],'product'[Subcategory],"Sales Total",SUM(sales[Sales Amount]))
D. SELECTCOLUMNS('sales,'product'[Category],'product'[Subcategory],sales[Sales Amount])

**Answer: C.**

Explanation
The answer is C.
You can use SUMMARIZE to create a summary of the input table grouped by the specified columns. You can alias an expression by using quotation marks such as "Sales Total". Also, note that you need to use the aggregation SUM() for the sales amount, or all sales lines will show.
In A, do not use DATATABLE. The DATATABLE function is used to build constant tables with code.
In B, the SUM() aggregation is missing on the sales amount field.
In D, do not use SELECTCOLUMNS. The SELECTCOLUMNS function adds a calculated column to a table and expects the input <column name> and <expression>.

**Question 8:**
**CASE 3**
**You work as a Power BI professional within your company's HR group. You are creating a data model to use for reporting within the group. As you start building relationships, you see there are issues connecting some of the tables.**
**What two fixes are required to get the relationships working in your data model?**

| Table Name | Column Name | Data Type |
|---|---|---|
| Employees | EmployeeID | Whole number |
| | Hire Date | Date |
| | GenderID | Whole number |
| | AgeID | Whole number |
| | Ethnicity | Text |
| | Relocation | Text |
| | HR Manager | Text |
| | Previous company | Text |
| | PayID | Percentage |
| | BUID | Whole number |
| PayType | PayID | Whole number |
| | Signing bonus | Fixed decimal |
| | Salary | Fixed decimal |
| AgeGroup | AgeID | Whole number |
| | AgeGroup | Text |
| BU | BUID | Text |
| | BU Name | Text |
| | Region | Text |
| Gender | GenderID | Whole number |
| | Gender | Text |

A. Change the data type of Employees[PayID] and hide Employees[Relocation] and Employees[HR Manager] fields
B. Change the data type of Employees[PayID] and BU[BUILD] to Whole Number
C. Ensure the cardinality between BU and Employees from Many to one (*:1) to Many to many (*:*)
D. Change the data type of Employees[PayID] and BU[BUILD] to Text

**Answer: B.**

Explanation
The answer is B.
You need to change the datatype of Employees[PayID] and BU[BUID] to Whole Number. If data types between tables do not match, you will not be able to create joins.
Answer A is incorrect as hiding fields does not help the relationship between tables.
Answer C is wrong as there is no need to change the BU relationship to Many to many
Answer D is incorrect as Text is the wrong data type, the correct data type is whole number

**Question 9:**
**CASE 3**
**You work as a Power BI professional within your company's HR group. The report you created for retention analysis worked fine in the development environment, but when deployed has performance issues.**
**Solution: Remove columns from the data model not used in reports**
**Does this solution meet the goal?**

| Table Name | Column Name | Data Type |
|---|---|---|
| Employees | EmployeeID | Whole number |
|  | Hire Date | Date |
|  | GenderID | Whole number |
|  | AgeID | Whole number |
|  | Ethnicity | Text |
|  | Relocation | Text |
|  | HR Manager | Text |
|  | Previous company | Text |
|  | PayID | Percentage |
|  | BUID | Whole number |
| PayType | PayID | Whole number |
|  | Signing bonus | Fixed decimal |
|  | Salary | Fixed decimal |
| AgeGroup | AgeID | Whole number |
|  | AgeGroup | Text |
| BU | BUID | Text |
|  | BU Name | Text |
|  | Region | Text |
| Gender | GenderID | Whole number |
|  | Gender | Text |

A. Yes
B. No.

**Answer: A.**

Explanation
The answer is A.
Removing unnecessary columns from the model will reduce the data model size and allow for improved refresh time.

**Question 10:**
**CASE 3**
**You work as a Power BI professional within your company's HR group. The report you created for retention analysis worked fine in the development environment, but when deployed has performance issues.**
**Solution: Hide columns and tables from the data model not used in reports**
**Does this solution meet the goal?**

| Table Name | Column Name | Data Type |
|---|---|---|
| Employees | EmployeeID | Whole number |
| | Hire Date | Date |
| | GenderID | Whole number |
| | AgeID | Whole number |
| | Ethnicity | Text |
| | Relocation | Text |
| | HR Manager | Text |
| | Previous company | Text |
| | PayID | Percentage |
| | BUID | Whole number |
| PayType | PayID | Whole number |
| | Signing bonus | Fixed decimal |
| | Salary | Fixed decimal |
| AgeGroup | AgeID | Whole number |
| | AgeGroup | Text |
| BU | BUID | Text |
| | BU Name | Text |
| | Region | Text |
| Gender | GenderID | Whole number |
| | Gender | Text |

A. Yes
B. No.

**Answer: B**

Explanation
The answer is B.
Hiding a column or a table will hide the items from the user in the Report view. The hidden columns and tables are still processed by Power BI and do not affect model size or performance.

**Question 11:**
**You find an interesting visualization using the Python programming language that you want to run in Power BI. What are the three steps required before you can use Python in Power BI?**
   A. Install Python on your local machine
   B. Enable R scripting
   C. Install the libraries matplotlib and pandas

D. Enable Python scripting

E. Install the libraries seaborn and keras

**Answer: A, C, D.**

Explanation
The answer is A, C and D.
The steps to get started with Python in Power BI are:
1. Install Python on your local machine
2. Install the libraries matplotlib and pandas
3. Enable Python scripting

Answer B is incorrect. R scripting is a separate language and has no relation with Python. Answer E is incorrect. While seaborn is used for data visualization, matplotlib and pandas are required libraries for Python integration. Note that keras is a deep learning library and is not used for data visualization.

**Question 12:**
**You are asked to optimize the performance of your data model. You have several intermediate queries that are not used for visualization and you have a large transactional table with a Date/Time field. What two optimizations should you do?**

A. Change all relationship cross filter directions to single

B. Split the Date/Time field into a separate Date column and a separate Time column

C. Turn off single select on slicers

D. Disable Power Query load on intermediary queries

**Answer: B, D.**

Explanation
The answer is B and D.
A Date/Time field has many unique or high cardinality values making optimization within the VertiPaq engine difficult. By splitting the Date/Time field into a separate Date and Time field, you reduce the uniqueness of the data and allow for greater storage optimization. Intermediate queries that are intended to support data integration with other queries should not be loaded into the model. To avoid loading the query to the model, ensure that you disable query load in these instances.

Answer A is not correct. You should use the relationship cross filter direction to enable reporting requirements.

Answer C is not correct. Single select works more efficiently than multi-select on slicers.

**Question 13:**
**You receive a new table to incorporate into your analysis in Power BI. You use Power Query to preview the data. For each of the following statements, select Yes if the statement is true. Otherwise, select No.**

| Statement | Yes | No |
|---|---|---|
| By default, Data Preview analyzes the first 5,000 rows in the dataset. | | |
| When you hover your mouse over column quality, you can see both number and percentage of valid, error and empty cells. | | |
| You can use the entire dataset for column profiling. | | |

    A. Yes / Yes / Yes
    B. No / Yes / Yes
    C. No / Yes / No
    D. No / No / Yes

**Answer: B.**

Explanation
The answer is B.
By default, Data Preview analyzes the first 1,000 rows in the dataset. When you hover your mouse over a column's data preview for column quality, you can see the number and percentage for valid / error / empty cells. You can change the Data Preview from the first 1,000 rows to the entire dataset.

**Question 14:**
**You are the Power BI administrator at your company which builds VR headsets. You need to assign appropriate workspace roles to your colleagues and must use the lowest permission necessary to accomplish the task. Which roles should you use for the below workspace requirements?**
    1. **Update and delete workspaces**
    2. **Publish apps**
    3. **Publish content to the workspace**

    A. Member / Member / Contributor
    B. Member! Member/Viewer
    C. Admin / Member/ Contributor
    D. Admin / Admin / Contributor

**Answer: C.**

Explanation
The answer is C.

An admin can update and delete workspaces. A member can publish apps, and a contributor can publish content to the workspace.

**Question 15:**
**You have a table of temperatures for various cities. Some cities use Fahrenheit, while others use Celsius. You need to write a DAX expression to create a new column called Category for the following conditions.**
**· If the value is greater than 80 and Units are F, then 'Hot'. Otherwise 'Not Hot'**
**· If the value is greater than 26 and Units are C, then 'Hot'. Otherwise 'Not Hot'**
**Complete the below DAX expression by replacing [VALUE]:**
**Category =**
**[VALUE] ( [VALUE] ( [VALUE] (Temperature[Value] > 80,Temperature[Units]="F"),**
**[VALUE] (Temperature[Value] > 26,Temperature[Units]="C") ),"Hot","Not Hot")**

| City | Value | Units |
|------|-------|-------|
| Austin | 90 | F |
| Baltimore | 79 | F |
| Boise | 76 | F |
| Calgary | 20 | C |
| Chicago | 72 | F |
| Detroit | 70 | F |
| Houston | 97 | F |
| Montréal | 27 | C |
| Nashville | 78 | F |
| Ottawa | 24 | C |

    A.  SWITCH/ AND / OR / AND
    B.  SWITCH /OR / OR / AND
    C.  IF / OR / AND / AND
    D.  IF / AND / OR / AND
    E.  WHILE / AND / OR / AND

**Answer: C.**

Explanation
The answer is C. The correct expression is:
IF( OR( AND(Temperature[Value] > 80,Temperature[Units]="F"), AND(Temperature[Value] > 26,Temperature[Units]="C") ),"Hot","Not Hot")
The expression begins with an IF statement. We know we have to test whether the Unit is F or C, so the first logical expression is an OR. Within the F and C check, we also have to check

54

whether the temperature is above a threshold. Since we have two logical items that must go together, we use an AND statement. If either the C or the F condition is true, the function will return 'Hot'. If the expression is false, then we return 'Not Hot'.

Answers A and B are incorrect. A switch statement needs the form of SWITCH(<expression>, <value1>, <result1>,<value2>,<result2> ...)

Answer E is incorrect. DAX has no WHILE function.

**Question 16:**
**Your boss has scrolled through the Theme Gallery on the website https://community.powerbi.com/.**
**She asks you to use a particular theme for your company's report in Power BI Service. How do you incorporate the theme in your report?**
- A. Download the JSON file and in Custom Dashboard theme > Upload JSON theme
- B. Download the CSS file and in Custom Dashboard theme > Upload CSS theme
- C. Download the PNG file and right-click on a tile > Upload PNG theme
- D. Download the PDF file and right-click on the dashboard > Upload PDF theme

**Answer: A.**

Explanation
The answer is A.
You can download a JSON file from the theme gallery. To import the theme into Power BI service, select Upload JSON theme in the Custom Dashboard theme window. Themes are only in JSON format. All other file formats such as CSS, PNG or PDF will not work.

**Question 17:**
**You are your company's Power BI expert. You know that data lineage shows you which data sources are used by which datasets. One of your colleagues says he cannot access data lineage. What could be two possible explanations for data lineage not working?**
- A. Only admins can see the lineage view
- B. You need a Power BI Pro license to see lineage view
- C. Lineage only works for DirectQuery datasets
- D. Lineage view is available only to users with higher than Viewer access to the workspace
- E. Each user needs to be granted lineage view permission in the tenant settings

**Answer: B, D.**

Explanation
The answer is B and D.
For lineage to work, you need to ensure you have a Power BI Pro license and you have access to the workspace. Furthermore, users must have an Admin, Member, or Contributor role in the workspace. Users with a Viewer role can't switch to lineage view.
Answer A is incorrect. Users with Admin, Member, or Contributor roles in the workspace can see lineage view.

Answer C is incorrect. Lineage is not limited to DirectQuery datasets.
Answer E is incorrect. You do not need to assign individual permissions for lineage view in the tenant settings.

## Question 18:

**You have a data set that shows employees and their bosses, as per the exhibit below. There is a field for each Employee called Employee_Name and a field for their boss Parent_Employee_Name. How would you create the Employee_Hierarchy column with a delimited hierarchy list in DAX?**

| EmployeeID | Employee_Name | Parent_EmployeeID | Parent_Employee_Name | Employee_Hierarchy |
|---|---|---|---|---|
| 111 | Steven May | | | Steven May |
| 2 | Nathan Jones | 111 | Steven May | Steven May \| Nathan Jones |
| 3 | Christian Salem | 2 | Nathan Jones | Steven May \| Nathan Jones \| Christian Salem |
| 4 | James Harmes | 3 | Christian Salem | Steven May \| Nathan Jones \| Christian Salem \| James Harmes |
| 5 | Chris Petracca | 3 | Christian Salem | Steven May \| Nathan Jones \| Christian Salem \| Chris Petracca |

A. PATHITEM(employees[Employee_Name], employees[Parent_Employee_Name])
B. RELATED(employees[Parent_Employee_Name], employees[Employee_Name])
C. CONCATENATE(employees[Parent_Employee_Name], employees[Employee_Name])
D. PATH(employees[Employee_Name], employees[Parent_Employee_Name])

**Answer: D.**

Explanation
The answer is D.
The PATH function is used to create a hierarchy. The PATH function returns a string that contains a delimited list, starting with the top/root of a hierarchy and ending with the bottom of the hierarchy.
Do not use PATHITEM. The PATHITEM() function returns the 'nth' item in the delimited list produced by the PATH function.
Do not use RELATED. The RELATED() function returns a related value from another table.
DO not use CONCATENATE. The CONCATENATE() function joins two text strings into one text string. We want a full hierarchy and not just a single concatenation.

## Question 19:

**You work for a computer accessories company and your data model contains the following tables:**
**1. Accessories table: 1k rows that are updated monthly**
**2. Sales table: 15M rows that are updated regularly with changes that need to be shown immediately**
**3. Date table: 10k rows that are updated rarely**
**For the three tables ABOVE, which storage mode should you use from the below options?**
- **Import**

- **DirectQuery**
- **Dual**

A. Accessories: Import / Sales: DirectQuery/ Date: Dual
B. Accessories: Import / Sales: DirectQuery/ Date: Import
C. Accessories: DirectQuery / Sales: Import I Date: DirectQuery

**Answer: B.**

Explanation
The answer is B.
For the accessories and date table you should use the import storage model. Imported tables with this setting are cached. Queries submitted to the Power BI dataset that return data from Import tables can be fulfilled only from cached data. The import method is used for static or low volume data.
The sales table should use the DirectQuery storage mode. Tables with this setting are not cached. Queries that you submit to the Power BI dataset from DirectQuery tables can be fulfilled only by executing on-demand queries to the data source.Use DirectQuery when you have a large data set with millions of rows that need to be shown immediately in the report.
You should not use the dual storage model. Dual storage tables can act as either cached or not cached, depending on the context of the query that's submitted to the Power BI database.

**Question 20:**
**You work for a consulting company that has a contract with a large government department. Part of the requirements for the report is to configure the page for use with a screen reader for sight-impaired users. What should you configure in your report such that the page follows a logical sequence?**
    A. Bookmarks
    B. Tab order
    C. Filters on all pages
    D. Layer order

**Answer: B.**

Explanation
The answer is B.
The tab order is used by keyboard users to navigate the report page. Screen reader and accessibility software follow the sequence of tab order.You should not use bookmarks on your report for this purpose. Bookmarks save the current filters and slicers, cross-highlighted visuals, sort order. You should not use Filters on all pages. Filters select a subset of your data and do not help with accessibility. You should not use layer order. The layer order is used to control the order in which visuals are shown and is used if you have visuals that overlap.

**Question 21:**

**You work at a sports betting company and have a table with US soccer scores and a second table with betting odds. Both tables share a common key called GameID. Your boss asks you to create a new combined table. Which transform should you use to create the dataset?**
  A. Append queries as new
  B. Append queries
  C. Merge queries as new
  D. Merge queries

**Answer: C.**

Explanation
The answer is C.
You should use the merge queries as a new transformation to create a new table with soccer scores and the betting odds. A merge query allows you to combine two or more tables into a single table based on a common column between the tables. This is similar to a JOIN in SQL.
You should not use append queries as new or append queries. An append query transformation combines tables with the same schema. This is similar to a UNION query in SQL. Since we want to add a column and the tables do not have the same schema we cannot use an append transformation.
You should not use merge queries since your boss specifically asked for a new combined table. You should use the merge queries as a new transformation.

**Question 22:**
**You work for a transportation company that uses Azure IoT devices to monitor the temperature within containers. The head of Supply Chain has asked you to create a dashboard for the streaming data from the IoT devices and you need to configure Power BI appropriately. For each of the following statements, select Yes if the statement is true. Otherwise, select No.**

| Statement | Yes | No |
|---|---|---|
| You can build report visuals using the data that flows in from the stream. | | |
| Visualize a streaming dataset by adding a dashboard tile. | | |
| Streaming data can make use of report functionality such as filtering. | | |

  A. No / Yes / No
  B. Yes / Yes / No
  C. No / No / Yes
  D. No / No / No

**Answer: A.**

Explanation
The answer is A.
Since there is no underlying database, you cannot build report visuals using the data that flows in from the stream. To visualize a streaming dataset, add a dashboard tile then select streaming data. You cannot use filtering with streaming data. Since there is no underlying database, you cannot make use of report functionality such as filtering, Power BI visuals, and other report functions.

**Question 23:**
**You are part of a planning team and are investigating the forecast accuracy across multiple plants, various products and a series of demand types (e.g. stable, seasonal, growing etc.) You use Power BI and know that there is a visual that can help you with the root cause of low forecast accuracy. Which visual should you choose?**
   A. Waterfall
   B. Treemap
   C. Key influencers
   D. Decomposition tree

**Answer: D.**

Explanation
The answer is D.
You should use the decomposition tree. A decomposition tree lets you visualize data across multiple dimensions. It automatically aggregates data and enables drilling down into your dimensions in any order. It also uses artificial intelligence, so you can ask it to find the next dimension to drill down into based on certain criteria, making it useful for root cause analysis.
You should not use a waterfall chart. A waterfall visual is used to show how an initial value is affected by a series of changes and does not help with root cause analysis.
You should not use a treemap. A treemap displays hierarchical data as a set of nested rectangles. Each level of the hierarchy is represented by a colored rectangle (branch) containing smaller rectangles (leaves). A treemap does not help with root cause analysis.
You should not use a key influencer's visual. A key influencers chart helps you understand the factors that drive a metric you're interested in. It analyzes your data, ranks the factors that matter, and displays them as key influencers. The key influencers rank factors and are not used for root cause analysis.

**Question 24:**
**You work for a baseball hat retailer and you need to create a table of the top 3 team names by the total number of transactions. You have a table called Hat Sales and another for Team. Select the proper DAX functions to correctly complete the formula by replacing the [VALUE] field:**

```
Top Hat Sales = [VALUE] ( 3,
[VALUE] ( HatSales, HatTeams[Team Name], "Transactions",
COUNT(HatSales[TransactionID])
), [Transactions],DESC)
```

| Table Name | Column Name |
|---|---|
| Hat Sales | TransactionID |
| | Date |
| | TeamID |
| | Units |
| | Amount |
| Team | TeamID |
| | Team Name |
| | Team Location |

    A. RANKX - CALCULATE
    B. TOPN - CALCULATE
    C. FILTER - SUMMARIZE
    D. TOPN - SUMMARIZE

**Answer: D.**

Explanation
The answer is D.
You can create a table of the top 3 Team Names by the count of transactions using TOPN. Within the function we can use SUMMARIZE to build a virtual table to give Team Name and Count of TransactionID. Lastly, since we want the top 3, we use DESC. If we wanted the bottom 3, we would use ASC.
Do not use RANKX. The RANKX function returns the rank of an expression evaluated in the current context in the list of values for the expression evaluated for each row in the specified table. RANKX does not expect a parameter such as 3 as the first argument.
Do not use CALCULATE since we want to create a virtual table. Use SUMMARIZE instead.
Do not use FILTER. The FILTER function returns a table that has been filtered and does not rank the rows.

**Question 25:**
**You import a large table from Excel into Power BI and you suspect there may be missing data. How would you find the percentage of empty cells in each column?**
    A. Column quality

B. Column profile
C. Show whitespace
D. Column distribution

**Answer: A.**

Explanation
The answer is A.
The Column quality checks the quality of the data in terms of Valid, Error & Empty and is expressed as a percentage.
Column profile provides a more in-depth look at the data in a column. Apart from the column distribution chart, it contains a column statistics chart. While the column profile provides the count of empty cells, it does not show a percentage of empty cells.
The whitespace feature in data preview shows whitespace and newline characters.
Column distribution provides a set of visuals underneath the names of the columns that showcase the frequency and distribution of the values in each of the columns.

**Question 26:**
**You work for a shoe distribution company and your firm uses Power BI for reporting. One of the reports you have created is exported as a PDF so the warehouse staff can check off items on a hard copy. Your company, however, has a policy that all exported reports need to be encrypted. How can you meet this requirement?**
A. Use Row Level Security (RLS)
B. Set the PDF options in the tenant settings
C. Configure the dataset build permission security options
D. Use sensitivity labels

**Answer: D.**

Explanation
The answer is D.
When you apply a sensitivity label to a report, Power BI automatically applies the label to the exported file and protects it according to the label's file encryption settings. This way, your data can remain protected, even when it leaves Power BI.
Do not use Row-level Security (RLS) for PDF exports. Row-level Security is used to restrict data access for given users by filtering the rows they see. Row-level does nothing to encrypt reports that are printed to PDF.
There are no PDF options in the tenant settings.
Do not use the dataset build permission security option. The dataset build permission allows other users in power BI Service to discover and reuse the dataset you've shared. The build permission does not protect any exported PDFs.

**Question 27:**

**You work for a share trading software company and have a dashboard for user trading times. The data set used for the analysis goes back seven years. When the data reloads, it takes excessive time as the full seven years are refreshed. How can you improve the dataset performance?**

A. Use an on-premises data gateway
B. Configure incremental refresh in Power BI Desktop and enable it in Power BI service
C. Enable incremental refresh directly in Power BI service
D. Manually refresh the database when users are not active

**Answer: B.**

Explanation
The answer is B.
With incremental refresh, the service dynamically partitions and separates data that needs to be refreshed frequently from data that can be refreshed less frequently. Table data is filtered using Power Query parameters with the names 'RangeStart' and 'RangeEnd,' defined using Power BI Desktop. Once the incremental refresh has been configured in Power BI Desktop, the dataset can be uploaded to Power BI service.
In answer A, an on-premise data gateway is used to access local files and does not help with optimizing the refresh process.
In answer C, incremental refresh cannot be configured directly in Power BI service. Incremental refresh must first be configured in Power BI Desktop.
Manually refreshing the dataset is not an efficient long term solution. Use incremental refresh instead.

**Question 28:**
**You are in Power Query Editor and you see the below highlighted in the red box. What data preview option is used to create these charts?**

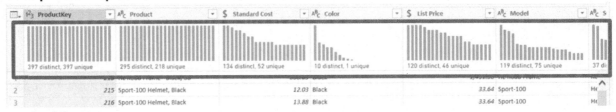

A. Monospace
B. Column distribution
C. Column quality
D. Column profile

**Answer: B.**

Explanation
The answer is B.
Column distribution shows the distribution of dal afro all columns and counts the number of distinct and unique items. Monospaced displays the data using a monospaced font.

Column quality shows the percentage of valid, error and empty values in a column. Column quality does not produce a graph.

Column profile shows statistics and the distribution of data for a single column. Column profile does not show all column charts at once.

## Question 29:

You have a data model with two key tables: Region and Shipping. There is a one-to-many relationship between the Region and the Shipping table. The model also has two row-level security roles named Region_Texas and Shipping_Mode The DAX filters for the two security roles are:

- Region_Texas filter is: Region[state] = "Texas"
- Shipping_Mode filter is: Shipping[mode] = "Rail"

If a manager is a member of both the Region_Texas and Shipping_Mode roles, what will they see in a report using this data model?

    A. The user will only see data for the state of Texas.
    B. The user will only see data for the rail shipping mode.
    C. The user will see data for which the state is Texas AND the shipping model is rail.
    D. The user will see data for which the state is Texas OR the shipping mode is rail.

## Answer: D.

Explanation
The answer is D.
When multiple roles are applied, a user will see filter 1 or filter 2. If the data has any states with Texas rows, the user will see those. If the data has the shipping mode of rail, then the user will also see those. The user is not restricted to both conditions, i.e. where a row is from Texas and has a rail shipping mode.
In answer A, the user will not see only Texas. They will also see rail shipments.
In answer B, the user will not see only rail shipments. They will also see Texas shipments.
In answer C, the user will see Texas OR rail shipments.

## Question 30:

You create an R visual in Power BI that has 500,000 rows. You notice that not all the data is shown and a message is displayed on the image. Your boss asks you the cause of this issue. What is the reason not all data is shown?

    A. You are using a version prior to 2.0 of the plotly library
    B. You are missing an R package
    C. The visual has too many rows
    D. The resolution is too high

## Answer: C.

Explanation
The answer is C.

R visuals for plotting are limited to 150,000 rows. If more than 150,000 rows are selected, only the top 150,000 rows are used and a message is displayed on the image. Additionally, the input data has a limit of 250 MB. The version of the plotly will not affect the number of rows. All R visuals are limited to 150,000 rows. If you are missing an R package, no image will show and you will only get an error message. R visuals are all displayed at a 72 DPI resolution. The resolution does not affect the number of rows that can be plotted.

**Question 31:**
**You have one report page with multiple visuals that is running slow, leading to complaints from users. What TWO solutions will help optimize your visuals?**
    A.  Don't use multiple colors on bar charts
    B.  Apply filters to reduce the max number of items that a visual displays
    C.  Replace the default visuals with custom visuals
    D.  Limit the use of bar charts
    E.  Limit the number of visuals on a particular report page to only what is necessary

**Answer: B, E.**

Explanation
The answer is B and E.
The more data that a visual needs to display, the slower that visual is to load. For instance, as a default, you may use the "Top N" filter to reduce the max number of items that a visual displays. It's highly recommended you limit the number of visuals on a particular report page to only what is necessary. Drillthrough pages and report page tooltips are great ways to provide additional details without jamming more visuals onto the page.
Answer A, using multiple colors on bar charts will not help optimize the visual.
In answer C, replacing the visual with custom visuals will not help optimize your report page.
Answer D, limiting the use of bar charts will not help optimize your report page.

**Question 32:**
**You are asked to create a category percentage measure that will reflect the values selected when using a slicer. In the output below, you will see that the Bikes category is not selected in the slicer and the category percentage reflects the current filter context. All category percentage values add to 100% of the filter context. You are given a measure that sums the sales called Sales Total. How would you create a category percentage measure in DAX?**

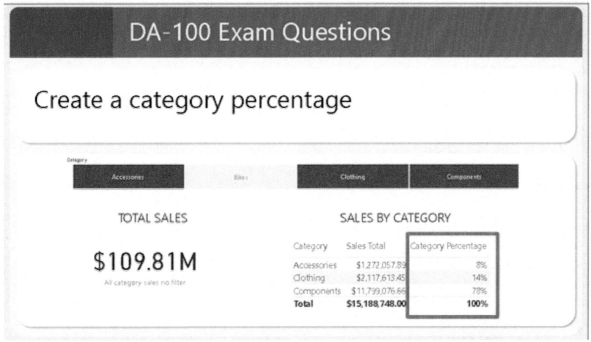

A.  VAR categoryTotal = CALCULATE([Sales Total],ALL('product' [Category])) VAR categoryPercentage = DIVIDE([Sales Total],categoryTotal) RETURN categoryPercentage

B.  VAR categoryTotal = [Sales Total] VAR categoryPercentage = DIVIDE([Sales Total],categoryTotal) RETURN categoryPercentage

C.  VAR categoryTotal = CALCULATE([Sales Total],ALLSELECTED('product'[Category])) VAR categoryPercentage = DIVIDE([Sales Total], categoryTotaL) RETURN categoryPercentage

D.  VAR categoryTotal = CALCULATE([Sales Total],REMOVEFILTERS('product'[Category])) VAR categoryPercentage = DIVIDE([Sales Total],categoryTotal) RETURN categoryPercentage

**Answer: C.**

Explanation
The answer is C.
The ALLSELECTED() function returns all the rows in a table, ignoring any filters that might have been applied inside the query, but keeping filters that come from outside. The categoryTotal value in this example equals $15.188 M and not the grand total of all category sales of $109.81 M. You can then use the DIVIDE() function to return the percentage of the category.
Answer A is incorrect since the ALL() function will ignore all filters and return the grand total of all category sales of $109.81 M.
Answer B is incorrect because no filtering of categories is applied.
Answer D is wrong as REMOVEFITLERS() is an alias for ALL() and returns the grand total of all category sales of $109.81 M.

**Question 33:**

You work for a Japanese auto company whose fiscal year starts April 1. You have a table called Cars with orders for cars. You need to create a common date for a data model using DAX, respecting the fiscal period. How should you create a date table using DAX?
   A. CALENDAR(4)
   B. CALENDAR( DATE (200031), DATE (YEAR (LASTDATE (Cars[OrderDate] )), 31, 3
   C. CALENDAR( DATE (YEAR ( FIRSTDATE ( Cars[OrderDate] ),4,1), DATE ( 2025, 12, 31 ))
   D. CALENDARAUTO(3)

**Answer: D.**

Explanation
The answer is D.
CALANDARAUTO() returns a table with a single column named "Date" containing a set of dates. The range of dates is calculated automatically based on data in the model. The parameter within the function gives the end month of the fiscal year. Since the fiscal year ends March 31, the parameter is 3.
In answer A, the CALENDAR() function expects a start and end date.
In answer B, the start date needs to be April / 1. A dynamic way would be to use FIRSTDATE and LASTDATE.
In answer C, the end date needs to be March / 31. A dynamic way would be to use FIRSTDATE and LASTDATE.

**Question 34:**
**You work in the spare parts department of an oil and gas company as a BI expert. The company has hundreds of parts, ten years of historic data, and hundreds of different order sizes from suppliers. You create a report in Power BI with aggregations for the following visuals:**
   - **A column chart of parts on the axis, but there are too many products showing**
   - **A stacked column chart of month number and order type, but too many months show**
   - **A histogram of supplier order sizes, but there are too many order sizes**
**You need to combine the data to make the visual more readable.**
**How should you combine the data? Select the GROUPING TYPE for each of the THREE solutions below from top to bottom.**
   1. **Combined the product into categories of product**
   2. **Combine the columns into 3 month number blocks**
   3. **Combine order sizes into 8 groups**

   A. LIST / BIN / LIST
   B. LIST / BIN / BIN
   C. BIN / LIST / LIST
   D. BIN / LIST / BIN

**Answer: B.**

Explanation
The answer is B.
You should use the List grouping type for text data such as products. You can combine a list of values into a category to simplify the data. You should use Binning to combine numeric data such as dates and quantity.

**Question 35:**
**You are analyzing basketball total points for the NBA for the year 2021. You have a measure [Points Total] which sums up the points and a date table with a year column. How should you complete the below DAX formula to effectively use it independently from any other filters set on the report page? Select the appropriate DAX function in place of [VALUE].**
**Sales 2021 =**
**CALCULATE(**
**[Points Total],**
**FILTER( [VALUE] ('Date'[Year]), 'Date'[Year] = 2021)**
**)**
    A. PATH
    B. ALL
    C. ALLEXCEPT
    D. RELATED

**Answer: B.**

Explanation
The answer is B.
The ALL() function returns all the rows in a table, or all the values in a column, ignoring any filters that might have been applied. The PATH() function returns a string that contains a delimited list of IDs, starting with the top/root of a hierarchy and ending with the specified ID. This does not help clear the filter context.
Do not use ALLEXCEPT() as the function returns a table except for those rows that are affected by the specified column filters.
Do not use RELATED() as the function is used to return a related value from another table.

**Question 36:**
**You want to use insights in Power BI Desktop to understand the increase from one quarter to the next in your sales column chart. Normally you would right-click the appropriate column and click on Analyze > Explain increase. However, this time insights does not appear to be available.**
**What are TWO possible reasons insights are not working?**
    A. You use hierarchies
    B. You use TOPN filters

C. You have filtered measures

D. You use a stacked column chart

**Answer: B, C.**

Explanation

The answer is B and C.

Insights are based on the change from the previous data point, and they aren't available when you select the first data point in a visual for several scenarios. Insights will not work with a scenario when you use TOPN filters or when you have filtered measures such as 'Total Sales for California.' Note that insights are also not supported for data sources such as DirectQuery and Live connect.

In answer A, hierarchies will work with insights.

In answer D, you can use a stacked column chart for insights.

**Question 37:**

**You work for an aerospace company in their satellite division. You build a workspace called 'satellite apps' in Power BI service that contains several reports and management level apps. You have a new analyst come on board and need to allow them to edit and publish reports. How would you achieve this goal?**

A. Configure the security group from Azure Active Directory

B. Add the user as a member in the role section of the 'satellite apps' workspace

C. In Power BI Desktop set Row Level Security (RLS)

D. Within the 'satellite apps' workspace, select update app

**Answer: B.**

Explanation

The answer is B.

Roles let you manage who can do what in the new workspaces, so teams can collaborate. New workspaces allow you to assign roles to individuals, and to user groups: security groups, Microsoft 365 groups, and distribution lists.

Answer A is not correct, we do not wish to configure a security group. We want to add a new role to the workspace.

Answer C is not correct, Row Level Security is a way to filter rows and does not enable editing and publishing

Answer D is not correct, update app is used to edit the content of an app and not assign edit and publish roles.

**Question 38:**

**You have a line chart that shows units manufactured by month. You want to add the on-time delivery metric for each month when you hover the mouse over a data point. How would you provide the additional piece of data?**

A. Add on-time delivery to the drillthrough fields

B. Add the on-time delivery column to the secondary values field
C. Add on-time delivery column to the tooltips field
D. Add the on-time delivery column to the small multiples field

**Answer: C.**

Explanation
The answer is C.
A tooltip is a way of providing more contextual information and detail to data points on a visual. When you hover over a data point, the tooltip data will show.
Answer A is incorrect. Drillthrough fields do not show on hover. When report readers use a drillthrough, they right-click a data point in other report pages, and drillthrough to the focused page to get details that are filtered to that context.
Answer B is incorrect. A secondary values field is used to show other numeric data on a line chart.
Answer B is incorrect. Small multiple is used to split your visuals into multiple smaller visuals, based on your selected fields.

**Question 39:**
**You create a Power BI report with a line chart as per the below exhibit. How do you add the dotted horizontal line for the mean values?**

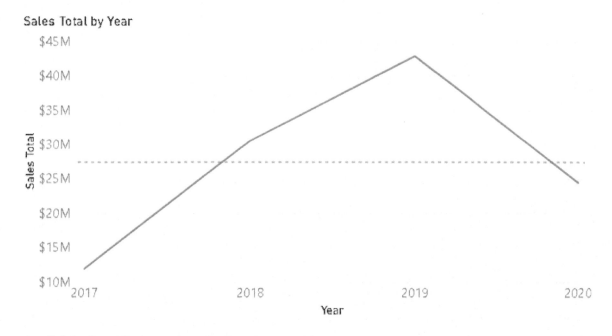

A. Add a fixed forecast line for the time series in the analytics pane
B. Add an Average line for Sales Total in the analytics pane
C. Add a trend line across years in the analytics pane
D. Add a min line in the analytics pane

**Answer: B.**

Explanation

The answer is B.

An average line will give the mean of the Sales Total. The average line is found in the analytics pane, and select Sales Total for the measure. Do not use a forecast line. A forecast line predicts future values in a time series and does not give mean values.

A trend line is a straight line that displays the trend in the data. A trend line would have a slope in this exhibit and does not give the mean of the data.

Do not use a min line. A minimum line gives the lowest point on the data, which is approximately $12M in the exhibit.

## Question 40:

**You have built several DAX measures. A senior Power BI member of your team asks you to improve the performance and readability of the below DAX expression? How would you achieve this goal?**

**Annual Sales Growth % =**
**DIVIDE(**
**([Sales] - CALCULATE([Sales], PARALLELPERIOD('Date'[Date], -12, MONTH))),**
**CALCULATE([Sales], PARALLELPERIOD('Date'[Date], -12, MONTH))**
**)**

    A. Replace DIVIDE with a simple divide calculation using the '/' symbol
    B. Instead of PARALLELPERIOD(), use DATEADD()
    C. Mark date table as date
    D. Use VARIABLES and a RETURN statement

**Answer: D.**

Explanation

The answer is D.

Variables and a return statement are used to improve the performance and readability of DAX expressions. The above expression could be re-written as the below:

Annual Sales Growth % =
VAR SalesPriorYear =
CALCULATE([Sales], PARALLELPERIOD('Date'[Date], -12, MONTH))
RETURN
DIVIDE(([Sales] - SalesPriorYear), SalesPriorYear)

In answer A, replacing the DIVIDE() function with '/' will not improve performance. The benefit of using the DIVIDE() function is it automatically handles divide by zero issues.

In answer B, using DATEADD() instead of PARALLELPERIOD() will not have an effect on performance and readability.

In answer C, marking the date table as date will not have an effect on the measure performance.

## Question 41:

You work for a forklift manufacturer. You are building a data model in Power BI and have a sales table as per the below exhibit. Within the sales table, there is a field called Model. How would you complete the DAX expression below to generate a Model table? What would you fill in for the [VALUE] fields starting from left to right?

Model Table = [VALUE] ( [VALUE] )

| Table Name | Column Name |
|---|---|
| Sales | TransactionID |
| | Date |
| | Category |
| | Subcategory |
| | Model |
| | Model Desc |
| | Units |
| | Amount |

A. CALCULATE / Sales[Model]
B. DISTINCT / Sales[Model]
C. CALCULATE / (Sales[Model] Model = "XPR")
D. DISTINCT / Sales[Model Desc]

**Answer: B.**

Explanation
The answer is B.
The DISTINCT() function returns a one column table that contains the distinct (unique) values in a column. Since we want a table for the models, use the column Sales[Model].
Answer A is incorrect. The CALCULATE function does not return a unique list of values. CALCULATE is used to evaluate an expression in a context modified by filters.
Answer C is incorrect. This expression filters the data for a Model "XPR" and does not give a list of unique Models.
Answer D is incorrect. We want a unique list of Model and not Model Desc.

**Question 42:**
**You work for an eCommerce company that sells ergonomic office products. You are tasked with creating a Power BI report from your company's transactional sales data in a table called 'ergoSales'. Before you do anything with the data, you want to check that there are no negative amounts in the 'ergoSales'[quantity] field.**

**What is the most efficient way to check your data for negatives before creating the data model?**

    A. Select Column profile and then click on 'ergoSales'[quantity]
    B. Select Column quality and then click on ergoSales'[quantity]
    C. Click on 'ergoSales'[quantity] and select replace values
    D. Create a custom column using a conditional statement to filter negatives out

**Answer: A.**

Explanation
The answer is A.
The Column profile view shows a column distribution chart of values as well as the minimum and maximum values. You can quickly see if your data has negative values by checking the distribution or by viewing the minimum value.
Answer B is incorrect. The Column quality view shows the percentage of Valid, Empty and Error cells.
Answer C is incorrect. Replacing values will not help you identify whether negative values exist.
Answer D is incorrect. Creating a custom filtered column does not help you quickly identify negative values. Selecting the Column profile is a more efficient technique.

**Question 43:**
**You work for a diesel engine company as an internal Power BI consultant. You have two tables as per the below exhibit. There are no unique values in either table. However, the tables are related by Model Name.**
**You need to create relationships in the data model to enable a visual containing data from both tables.**
**How would you model these two tables in the most efficient manner?**

| Table Name | Column Name |
|---|---|
| ConnectingRod | RodID |
| | Manufacture Date |
| | Supplier Name |
| | Model Name |

| CyclinderHead | CylinderID |
| --- | --- |
| | Manufacture Date |
| | Factory Name |
| | Model Name |

A. Set the relationship between the two tables as one-to-one
B. Set the relationship between the two tables as many-to-many
C. Create a bridging table using unique IDs and create two one-to-many relationships
D. Set the relationship between the two tables as one-to-many

**Answer: B.**

Explanation
The answer is B.
You should set the relationship between the ConnectingRod and CylinderHead table to many-to-many using the Model Name. A man-to-many relationship does not need unique values in either of the tables in the relationship.
You should not create a one-to-one relationship between the tables. A one-to-one relationship requires unique values on both sides of the relationship.
You should not build a bridging table when you can use a many-to-many relationship. A bridging table was the only means to create a many-to-many relationship in legacy versions of Power BI. However, current versions of Power BI support a many-to-many relationship, a far more efficient method that uses less data.
You should not use a one-to-many relationship. A one-to-many relationship is used when one table has unique values and the other does not have unique values. Since both tables do not have unique values, use a many-to-many relationship.

**Question 44:**
**You work for a manufacturing company with a metric called Supplied in Full on Time (SIFOT). In Power BI, you have built a dashboard to help management keep track of key summary data and metrics. One of your visuals is a gauge chart that shows the SIFOT values. The management team wants a notification to be sent when SIFOT drops below 85%. You need to configure email alerts to management when this happens. Which four actions should you perform to create this alert?**
A. Select + Add alert rule, ensure the Active slider is set to On
B. In the alert conditions choose 'below' and enter in a value of 85
C. Choose More options on the SIFOT gauge visual and select Manage alerts
D. In the dropdown for notification type, select email
E. In the alert conditions choose 'below' and enter in a value of 0.85
F. Check the 'Send me email too' and then save and close

**Answer: A, C, E, F.**

Explanation
The answer is A, C, E and F.
The steps required to set an email alert are:
1. Choose More options on the SIFOT gauge visual and select Manage alerts
2. Select + Add alert rule, ensure the Active slider is set to On
3. In the alert conditions choose 'below' and enter in a value of 0.85
4. Check the 'Send me an email too 'and then save and close

You should not set the alert condition with a value of 85. Power BI will multiply this value by 100 when calculating a percentage value.
There is no dropdown for a notification type. By default Power BI will send a notification in the notification center. To receive an email as well, you must use the 'Send me an email too' checkbox.

**Question 45:**
**You are the head of analytics for a software company, and you want to understand the importance of factors that drive sales in your pre-sales team. What visual in Power BI can help you achieve your goal?**
    A. Custom R Dumbell Plot
    B. Q&A
    C. Decomposition Tree
    D. Key Influencers

**Answer: D.**

Explanation
The answer is D.
A Key Influencers chart will help you understand the factors that drive a metric you're interested in e.g. sales. It analyzes your data, ranks the factors that matter, and displays them as key influencers.
You should not use a Custom R Dumbell Plot. A Dumbell plot is used to visualize relative positions (like growth and decline) between two points in time.
You should not use a Q&A visual. A Q&A visual is used to interrogate data using natural language algorithms.
You should not use a Decomposition Tree. A Decomposition tree lets you visualize data across multiple dimensions and is useful for root cause analysis.

**Question 46:**
**You are editing the 'Model' column in a 'product' table Power Query. You need to replace instances of 'LL Road Frame' with 'JJ Roadster' and the previous step is 'Changed Type.' What M code functions would you use for the two [VALUE] fields?**
**= Table. [VALUE] (#"Changed Type","LL Road Frame","JJ**

**Roadster",Replacer. [VALUE],{"Model"})**

   A. ReplaceValue / ReplaceText
   B. Replace Rows / ReplaceText
   C. ReplaceText / ReplaceValue
   D. ReplaceRows / ReplaceValue

**Answer: A.**

Explanation
The answer is A.
Table.ReplaceValue replaces an oldValue with newValue in the specified columns of the table.
Since we are replacing one string with another, use Replacer.ReplaceText. Do not use
ReplaceRows. ReplaceRows replaces the specified range of rows with a provided row.
Do not use ReplaceValue. When replacing strings use Replacer.ReplaceText and for numbers
use Replacer.ReplaceValue

**Question 47:**

**You work in the marketing division for a sports apparel company. You have a sales fact
table and multiple dimension tables as per the below exhibit. The head of marketing
wants to encourage self-service analytics within the company and asks that you set up
Q&A in the reports. Which of the following configurations will allow Q&A to work in your
data model?**

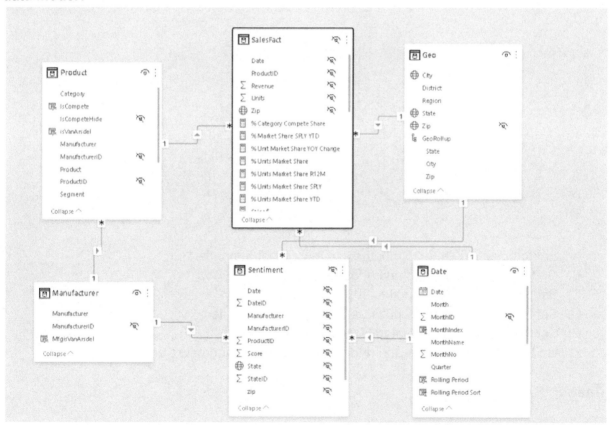

A. Object level security with any type of data source
B. Import
C. Composite models
D. Reporting Services

**Answer: B.**

Explanation
The answer is B.
Power BI currently supports Import mode, Live connect to Azure Analysis Services , Live connect to SQL Server Analysis Services (with a gateway) and Power BI datasets. Q&A does not support object level security with any type of data source, composite models and reporting services.

**Question 48:**
**You have sales data by day in a time series chart and need to produce a 25 day forecast with a 90% confidence interval as per the below exhibit. There are some data anomalies in the last 5 days of data that you want to ignore for the forecast. Select the THREE actions required to create the forecast.**

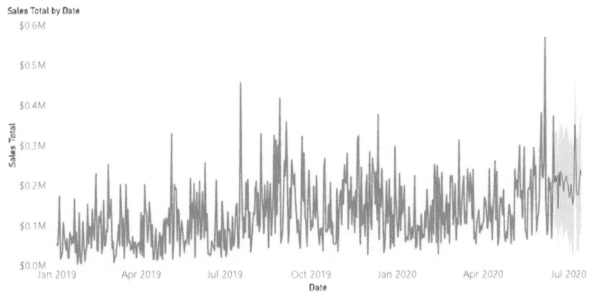

A. Set forecast length to 25 months and ignore last 5 months
B. Go to the analytics pane and under forecast select '+ Add'
C. Set the seasonality interval to 90% and click on apply
D. Set forecast length to 25 points and ignore last 5 points
E. Set the confidence interval to 90% and click on apply
F. Go to the analytics pane and under forecast select 'Add new trend'

**Answer: B, D, E.**

Explanation

76

The answer is B, D and E.
The steps to create a forecast with the above requirements are:
1. Go to the analytics pane and under forecast select '+ Add'
2. Set forecast length to 25 points and ignore the last 5 points
3. Set the confidence interval to 90% and click on apply

In answer A, do not use 25 months as the data is given in days.
In answer C, do not use seasonality. We want a confidence interval of 90%.
In answer F, there is no 'Add new trend' button. Use the '+ Add' button

## Question 49:
You have a busy report page called Sales and decide to use a detailed chart in a separate page using the drill through feature. The Sales page shows a visual of total sales by month. When you click on drill through on the sales by month chart, it should redirect to a detail page called Sales Detail that shows sales for the selected month by category. The Sales Detail page should also preserve the filters from the original sales page. What FOUR actions should you perform?
A. On the Sales Detail page, under drill through option add month as the drill through field
B. On the Sales page, under drill through option add month as the drill through field
C. Create a new page called Sales Detail
D. On the Sales Detail page under Drill through, toggle Keep all filters on
E. Create a table visual to show total sales by month and category
F. On the Sales page under Drill through, toggle Keep all filters on

**Answer: A, C, D, E.**

Explanation
The answer is A,C,D,E.
The correct steps to create a drill through are:
1. Create a new page called Sales Detail
2. Create a table visual to show total sales by month and category
3. On the Sales Detail page, under drill through option add month as the drill through field
4. On the Sales Detail page under Drill through, toggle Keep all filters on

Answer B and F are incorrect. The drill through options should be set on the Sales Detail page and not on the first Sales page. Once the drill through has been configured on the Sales Detail page, Power BI will automatically allow you to right-click on a month on the Sales page and select Drill through.

## Question 50:
You are asked to present your findings on your company's warehousing performance across several years. You have a number of column and line charts and a date slicer. You decide you will create a presentation using Power BI and will create a narrative using the date slicer. What should you do to save the views across different years for your presentation?
A. Create page level filters and create a new groups

B. Filter the charts using the date slicer, then create bookmarks
C. Create drill throughs for each of the warehouse charts
D. Create report level filters and create a new groups

**Answer: B.**

Explanation
The answer is B.
Bookmarks capture the current state of a report page. Bookmarks save the current slicers, filters, cross-highlighted visuals and sort order. You can get back to an exact state when you select your saved bookmark. This makes bookmarks ideal for creating a presentation in Power BI. Page-level filters cannot be saved into a new group. Groups are used to create bins or categories in lists.
Drill throughs do not save a state for a presentation. Drill throughs are used to dive into a detailed page, while keeping the source page filters. Report level filters cannot be saved into a new group. Groups are used to create bins or categories in lists.

**Question 51:**
**You work in a marketing department as a Power BI professional. You are asked to create three different types of visuals for the marketing department. Which visualization should you use for the below three requirements?**
**1. Show progress of conversion rates against a target**
**2. Identify outliers in sentiment scores**
**3. Show the factors that influence sentiment scores**
    A. KPI / Waterfall / Treemap
    B. Card / Scatter / Funnel
    C. KPI / Scatter / Key influencers
    D. Card / Funnel / Scatter

**Answer: C.**

Explanation
The answer is C.
A KPI chart shows the progress against a target, a scatter chart can help visually identify outliers and Key influencers can show the factors that drive a metric you're interested in.
A waterfall chart is used to understand how an initial value is affected by a series of positive and negative changes.
A Treemap chart displays hierarchical data as a set of nested rectangles.
A Funnel chart helps you visualize a linear process that has sequential connected stages.
A Card visual shows a single number such as a total.

**Question 52:**
**You have built a report with multiple visuals for your food manufacturing company. As many senior members are often on the road, they ask that the reports be available for**

mobile devices. You need to optimize the report for mobile devices for the most critical visuals. Which three things can you do to optimize reports for mobile?

    A.  Set slicers to be responsive
    B.  Add the most important visuals to the mobile canvas
    C.  Set the page size as tablet or smartphone
    D.  Resize the visuals to fit the mobile canvas
    E.  Add haptic feedback (vibration) for when a user taps a visual
    F.  Remove chart axes

**Answer: A, B, D.**

Explanation
The answers are A, B and D.
Setting slicers to be responsive means that the slicer will automatically adjust its size in the mobile app. Add the most important visuals to the canvas for senior members of the company. You can add a visual by dragging it onto the canvas and remove it by clicking on the cross in the right corner. Lastly, you can resize a visual by dragging out the sides or by dragging a corner.
You cannot set a specific page size for a tablet or smartphone. The mobile app uses a single mobile layout. You cannot add haptic feedback (vibration) to a report visual.
You cannot separately remove a chart's axes for the mobile view. If you change a chart's axes, it is reflected in both the Desktop and mobile view.

**Question 53:**
**You work for a College Football team as a Power BI sports analyst. You have built a report in Power BI Desktop that contains many visuals. The coaching team is pleased with the content of the visuals but wants the colors to match the college's color style guide. What should you do?**

    A.  Adjust the report CSS file
    B.  Customize the current theme
    C.  Change the fonts on each text box
    D.  Change the colors on each visual

**Answer: B.**

Explanation
The answer is B.
In Power BI Desktop, navigate to View > Themes > Customize the current theme. In the theme's settings, you can change colors and fonts for all visuals.
In answer A, Power BI does not have a CSS file for themes. When importing themes, however, you can use a JSON file.
In answer C, do not change the fonts individually. All fonts can be changed by adjusting the current theme.

In answer D, do not change colors individually. All colors can be changed by adjusting the current theme.

**Question 54:**

**You work for a microbrewery as head of data visualization. You have a Power BI data model that relies on several Excel files that reside on your company's internal server. You are emailed a new Excel workbook from the CEO that contains updated data. You place the new Excel workbook on your server and append the text 'v1.2' to the name. For each of the following statements, select Yes if the statement is true. Otherwise, select No.**

| Statement | Yes | No |
| --- | --- | --- |
| The new Excel file must have the same structure as the original workbook. | | |
| The new Excel workbook will only work if it has the exact same name and path as the previous file. | | |
| You can refresh the local Excel file by pressing F5 in Power BI. | | |

    A. Yes / No / No
    B. Yes / No / Yes
    C. No / Yes / Yes
    D. No / Yes / No

**Answer: A.**

Explanation
The answer is A.
The new Excel file must have the same schema as the original Excel file. If there are fewer columns, more columns or differently named columns, the report will not work.
The new file can have a different name and a different file path. In Power Query Editor, you can change the source path and filename for the new file.
You cannot refresh the local Excel file by pressing F5 in Power BI. If you need to be able to refresh the data for reports published to Power BI Server, you will need a data gateway. Otherwise, you can host the file on a cloud platform such as OneDrive.

**Question 55:**

**Your company uses Power BI Premium and your manager wants to create printed invoices. However, the reports must fit perfectly on a page. What would you suggest to your manager?**
    A. Change the page view in Power BI Desktop
    B. Use paginated reports

C. Use gridlines and snap to grid
D. Use lock objects

**Answer: B.**

Explanation
The answer is B.
Paginated reports are designed to be printed or shared. They are called paginated because they are formatted to fit well on a page and are sometimes called 'pixel perfect.'
In answer A, changing the page view will not ensure the printed report will be consistent.
In answer C, gridlines and snap to grid will help align the report, but it is uncertain that you will be able to print the report to fit perfectly on a page.
In answer D, lock objects are used to keep an object in place while you are giving a presentation or interacting with the report elements.

**Question 56:**
**You work in a shoe company's reporting team and have been tasked with building a Power BI report showing procurement analytics. You have an on-premises Microsoft SQL Server database that you use to build the procurement report using a DirectQuery connection. You thoroughly test the report and then upload it to Power BI Service. However, once in Power BI Service, the visualizations no longer work. How would you solve this problem?**
A. Change the permissions on your Microsoft SQL Server database
B. Upgrade your Power BI Desktop
C. Install an on-premise data gateway
D. Install Power BI Report Builder

**Answer: C.**

Explanation
The answer is C.
An on-premises data gateway is a software that you install in an on-premises network. The gateway facilitates access to data in that network.
In answer A, changing the permissions on Microsoft SQL will not allow Power BI Service access. A gateway is needed.
In answer B, upgrading Power BI Desktop will not assist in the power BI Service connection to your local SQL Server.
In answer D, Power BI Report Builder is a tool for authoring paginated reports that you can publish to the Power BI service. This helps you create 'pixel perfect reports' but will not help you connect to a local SQL Server database.

# Chapter 4: PL 300 Mock Test 2

**Question 1:**
**CASE 1**
You work as a BI analyst for a software company that allows users to manipulate images online. You have built a report that shows the conversion from free customers to premium customers. Your boss has asked you to provide a filter for the 'marketing' industry.
**Solution:**
- Apply a filter on all pages of the report for the 'marketing' industry
- Share the report
- Mark share report with current filters and slicer options

**Does this solution meet the requirements?**

    A. Yes
    B. No.


**Question 2:**
**CASE 1**
You work as a BI analyst for a software company that allows users to manipulate images online. You have built a report that shows the conversion from free customers to premium customers. Your boss has asked you to provide a filter for the 'marketing' industry.
**Solution:**
- Create a text parameter for industry
- Set the parameter equal to 'marketing'
- Create a query parameter on the industry column

**Does this solution meet the requirements?**

    A. Yes
    B. No.


**Question 3:**
**CASE 1**
You work as a BI analyst for a software company that allows users to manipulate images online. You have built a report that shows the conversion from free customers to premium customers. Your boss has asked you to provide a filter for the 'marketing' industry.
**Solution:**
- Add a slicer to the report and select the 'marketing' industry
- Sync slicers to all relevant pages of the report

**Does this solution meet the requirements?**

    A. Yes

    B. No


## Question 4:
**CASE 2**

You work for a financial institution, and you have built a data model and report in Power BI desktop. The report ran fine during testing, but when in production, users are complaining of performance issues. How can you improve the model's performance?

Solution: Hide intermediate tables in the model view

Does this help improve performance?

    A. Yes

    B. No


## Question 5:
**CASE 2**

You work for a financial institution, and you have built a data model and report in Power BI desktop. The report ran fine during testing, but when in production, users are complaining of performance issues. How can you improve the model's performance?

Solution: Convert source PO text column into a number by removing prefix, e.g. 'PO12399' to 12399

Does this help improve performance?

    A. Yes

    B. No.


## Question 6:
**CASE 2**

You work for a financial institution, and you have built a data model and report in Power BI desktop. The report ran fine during testing, but when in production, users are complaining of performance issues. How can you improve the model's performance?

Solution: Remove unnecessary columns

Does this help improve performance?

    A. Yes

    B. No


## Question 7:
**CASE 3**

You have the schema for the tables used in a bicycle franchise. In your role as a BI consultant, you have been asked to generate some insights from the data.

**Company data schema:**

| Table Name | Column Name | Data Type |
|---|---|---|
| Sales | CustomerKey | Whole number |
| | Order Quantity | Fixed decimal |
| | OrderDate | Date |
| | OrderDateKey | Whole number |
| | ProductKey | Whole number |
| | Sales Amount | Fixed decimal |
| | SalesOrderLineKey | Whole number |
| | SalesTerritoryKey | Whole number |
| | UnitPrice | Fixed decimal |
| Sales orders | Channel | Text |
| | Sales Order | Text |
| | Sales Order Line | Text |
| | SalesOrderLineKey | Whole number |
| Product | Category | Text |
| | Color | Text |
| | ListPrice | Fixed decimal |
| | Model | Text |
| | Product | Text |
| | ProductKey | Text |
| | SKU | Text |
| | Standard Cost | Fixed decimal |
| | Subcategory | Text |
| Date | Date | Date |
| | Day Number | Whole number |
| | Month Number | Whole number |
| | Year | Whole number |
| Customer | CustomerKey | Text |
| | Name | Text |
| | Post Code | Whole number |

**You are asked to create a visualization for the sales by product. However, what should you do before creating a relationship?**

    A. Change the datatype of Sales[ProductKey] to fixed decimal

    B. Create a calculated column of Product[ProductKey]

    C. Change the datatype of Product[ProductKey] to whole number

    D. Create a measure for the sum of Sales[Order Quantity]

**Question 8:**
**CASE 3**
You have the schema for the tables used in a bicycle franchise. In your role as a BI consultant, you have been asked to generate some insights from the data.
Company data schema:

| Table Name | Column Name | Data Type |
|---|---|---|
| Sales | CustomerKey | Whole number |
| | Order Quantity | Fixed decimal |
| | OrderDate | Date |
| | OrderDateKey | Whole number |
| | ProductKey | Whole number |
| | Sales Amount | Fixed decimal |
| | SalesOrderLineKey | Whole number |
| | SalesTerritoryKey | Whole number |
| | UnitPrice | Fixed decimal |
| Sales orders | Channel | Text |
| | Sales Order | Text |
| | Sales Order Line | Text |
| | SalesOrderLineKey | Whole number |
| Product | Category | Text |
| | Color | Text |
| | ListPrice | Fixed decimal |
| | Model | Text |
| | Product | Text |
| | ProductKey | Text |
| | SKU | Text |
| | Standard Cost | Fixed decimal |
| | Subcategory | Text |
| Date | Date | Date |
| | Day Number | Whole number |
| | Month Number | Whole number |
| | Year | Whole number |
| Customer | CustomerKey | Text |
| | Name | Text |
| | Post Code | Whole number |

**The product table's color column has abbreviations as well as names. For instance, there is both Black and BLK. What do you need to do to ensure consistency in the color column?**

    A. Export the table to Excel
    B. Use replace values in the transform ribbon in Power Query Editor
    C. Edit the source applied step in M code
    D. Remove duplicates in Power Query Editor

**Question 9:**
**CASE 3**
**You have the schema for the tables used in a bicycle franchise. In your role as a BI consultant, you have been asked to generate some insights from the data.**
**Company data schema:**

| Table Name | Column Name | Data Type |
|---|---|---|
| Sales | CustomerKey | Whole number |
| | Order Quantity | Fixed decimal |
| | OrderDate | Date |
| | OrderDateKey | Whole number |
| | ProductKey | Whole number |
| | Sales Amount | Fixed decimal |
| | SalesOrderLineKey | Whole number |
| | SalesTerritoryKey | Whole number |
| | UnitPrice | Fixed decimal |
| Sales orders | Channel | Text |
| | Sales Order | Text |
| | Sales Order Line | Text |
| | SalesOrderLineKey | Whole number |
| Product | Category | Text |
| | Color | Text |
| | ListPrice | Fixed decimal |
| | Model | Text |
| | Product | Text |
| | ProductKey | Text |
| | SKU | Text |
| | Standard Cost | Fixed decimal |
| | Subcategory | Text |

| Date | Date | Date |
|------|------|------|
| | Day Number | Whole number |
| | Month Number | Whole number |
| | Year | Whole number |
| Customer | CustomerKey | Text |
| | Name | Text |
| | Post Code | Whole number |

**When reviewing the customer table, you find that some of the postcodes appear to be missing. For instance '0800' does not seem to exist. What do you need to do to ensure all the Postcodes from the original data are in your model?**

    A. Use 'add columns from examples' to fix discrepancies

    B. Use 'transform' and then adjust the rounding

    C. Go to the transform ribbon and click on 'Use first row as header'

    D. Make sure the postcode data type is 'text' and not 'whole number'

**Answer: D.**

Explanation

The answer is D. If the original data uses '0' as a prefix for some post codes, converting to a whole number will remove the zero. For instance '0800' becomes 800. To prevent losing this data, change the postcode data type to 'text' in the applied step 'Changed Type.' Note that column profiling is based on the first 1000 rows and if Power BI does not see any cases of zero prefixes, the tool will assume the column is a whole number.

You should not use the add columns from examples as the issue is in the data type conversion. You should not adjust the rounding of the postcode number. The problem is at the start of the number and not the end of the number. Using the first row as header addresses the column name and not the data type.

**Question 10:**
**CASE 3**
**You have the schema for the tables used in a bicycle franchise. In your role as a BI consultant, you have been asked to generate some insights from the data.**
**Company data schema:**

| Table Name | Column Name | Data Type |
|------------|-------------|-----------|
| Sales | CustomerKey | Whole number |
| | Order Quantity | Fixed decimal |
| | OrderDate | Date |
| | OrderDateKey | Whole number |
| | ProductKey | Whole number |
| | Sales Amount | Fixed decimal |

| | SalesOrderLineKey | Whole number |
|---|---|---|
| | SalesTerritoryKey | Whole number |
| | UnitPrice | Fixed decimal |
| Sales orders | Channel | Text |
| | Sales Order | Text |
| | Sales Order Line | Text |
| | SalesOrderLineKey | Whole number |
| Product | Category | Text |
| | Color | Text |
| | ListPrice | Fixed decimal |
| | Model | Text |
| | Product | Text |
| | ProductKey | Text |
| | SKU | Text |
| | Standard Cost | Fixed decimal |
| | Subcategory | Text |
| Date | Date | Date |
| | Day Number | Whole number |
| | Month Number | Whole number |
| | Year | Whole number |
| Customer | CustomerKey | Text |
| | Name | Text |
| | Post Code | Whole number |

**You have been asked to add a column for profit, revenue – price. What steps do you need to do to calculate profit in the model?**

    A. Unpivot the Unit Price column -> Create custom column named Profit -> Set formula Sales Amount — (Order Quantity UnitPrice)

    B. Create custom column named Profit -> Set formula Sales Amount —(Order Quantity * UnitPrice) -> Set the data type to Fixed decimal

    C. Duplicate the Order Quantity Column -> Create a new column and multiply duplicated column by UnitPrice-> Create custom column named Profit

    D. Create a Group By on SalesOrderLineKey -> Sum by Sales Amount and rename Profit -> Subtract Unit Price

**Question 11:**

**You have some new staff joining your Power BI team. To help them get started in Power BI Desktop, you want to create a way for them to connect to the data sources that you are using in your project. All they will need to do to connect to the data is enter their user credentials to authenticate. How can you achieve this?**

A. Create a dynamic M query
B. Use an Excel Macro to build connections
C. Create a PBIDS file with your key data sources
D. Create a template in lineage view

## Question 12:

You use an R script to build a custom visual. However, you find that you cannot see data marked 'N/A' and you are getting an error when importing your data as a list. What could be TWO reasons for these issues?

A. 'NA' is transformed into 'NULL' by Power BI
B. You have not used the correct R version
C. Power BI only supports R dataframes
D. You need to first install the library 'tidyr'

## Question 13:

You have an inactive relationship between your date table and your shipping table. How would you use an inactive relationship in a measure?

A. Use the LOOKUPVALUE() function
B. Delete the active relationship and make the new relationship active
C. Use the USERELATIONSHIP() function
D. Change the crossfilter direction to both in the modeling tab

## Question 14:

Your client has asked you whether you can create data alerts for all of the key visuals on your dashboard. Which two visuals can you NOT create a data alert for?

A. Funnel chart
B. KPI chart
C. Stacked column chart
D. Gauge chart

## Question 15:

You build a key influencer visual and you want to see how sales amount is affected by product category and product color. How do you complete the three fields below?

Visualizations >

Analyze

Add data fields here

Explain by

Add data fields here

Expand by

Add data fields here

A. Analyze -> Sales[Sales Quantity]; Explain by -> Product[Category], Product[Color]
B. Analyze -> Sales[Sales Amount]; Expand by -> Product[Category], Product[Model]
C. Analyze -> Sales[Sales Quantity]; Explain by -> Product[Category]; Expand by ->Product[Color]
D. Analyze -> Sales[Sales Amount]; Explain by -> Product[Category], Product[Color]


**Question 16:**
**You work for NASA's Supply Chain division. NASA purchases parts for the international space station. There are two key tables: SpaceStationInventory and DateTable. The SpaceStationInventory table contains the inventory counts for the parts and the date of the counts. The DateTable is a date table you created using M code. The Supply Chain division works Monday to Friday and is closed on state and federal holidays. As senior BI specialist you have been tasked to show the inventory level for the international space station warehouse on the last day of each month. Which DAX function will meet your requirement?**

A. CALCULATE( SUM(SpaceStationInventory[Inventory Count]), LASTDATE(DateTable[Date])
B. CLOSINGBALANCEMONTH(SUMX(SpaceStationInventory[Inventory Count]), SpaceStationInventory[Date])
C. CALCULATE(SUM(SpaceStation Inventory[Inventory Count]), LASTDATE(SpaceStationInventory[Date])
D. CALCULATE(SUM(SpaceStation Inventory[Inventory Count]), FILTER(SpaceStationInventory, SpaceStationInventory[Inventory Count] = MAX(SpaceStationInventory[Inventory Count]))

**Question 17:**
You work for an electric car manufacturer and you need to import a Supplier table into your data model. The Supplier table lists the supplier id, full name, short name and address. When reviewing the data in Power BI, you want to check the distinct and unique rows for each column.
- A. Column profile
- B. Monospaced
- C. Column distribution
- D. Show whitespace
- E. Column quality


**Question 18:**
You work for a large multinational company that has 23 departments. You have been tasked with creating a report with all the first aid trained staff . You need to create the same report for each department. How can you create the same report for each department in the most efficient manner?
- A. Create separate Power BI Desktop report for each department and email the PBIX
- B. Add a parameter to the report to filter department
- C. Create a separate workspace for each department and create a report in each
- D. Create a separate dataset for each department and add a separate report


**Question 19:**
You have produced reports for a space tourism startup. The founder is thrilled with the Power BI service setup. However, he has some questions on how to promote and secure the datasets to other users in the company. His three requirements are below:
1. When Power BI Service launches, I want the competition report to be displayed on their screen.
2. For the financial dashboard, I want the classification of the data clearly displayed.
3. I want you to highlight particular reports because it is valuable and worthwhile for others to use. I also don't want you to ask permission from the Power BI Admin each time.

For the above requirements, them as either:
- **Certified**
- **Promoted**
- **Featured**
- **Sensitivity Label**

- A. Promoted / Certified I Featured
- B. Sensitivity Label / Featured / Promoted
- C. Featured / Sensitivity Label / Promoted
- D. Certified / Sensitivity Label / Promoted

**Question 20:**

**You work for an electric scooter manufacturer. You have a report with five pages, and you have been asked to filter all five pages when you select a particular scooter category on the first page. What are the two ways you could do this?**

    A. Add a page level filter on all five pages

    B. Create a report level filter using category in the 'Filter all pages well

    C. Use a single button and set the action type to bookmark

    D. Select paginated report and configure the settings

    E. Create a slicer for category on each page and then Sync slicers on all pages

**Question 21:**

**A colleague built a Power BI desktop report. Your colleague imported a flat file into Power BI from his local machine. You have inherited the Power BI report and you need to update the source for the file. How would you go about this?**

    A. On the home ribbon, click on properties and change the file path

    B. Click on the Applied step 'source and click on the cog to change the file path

    C. On the home ribbon, click on manage -> then file, then change the file path

    D. Click on the Applied step 'changed type' and click on the cog in the corner to change the file location

**Question 22:**

**A colleague calls you for help. She wants to build an app in Power BI and asks you how to publish the app. What are the three most important parts of publishing an app? Select THREE from the below.**

    A. On the permissions tab, decide who has access to the app

    B. On the title tab, fill in the name and description to help people find the app

    C. Before releasing the app, create a digital signature, so people know who built the app

    D. On the navigation tab, select the content to be visible in the app

    E. Click the Sync to organization button

    F. On the setup tab, fill in the name and description to help people find the app

**Question 23:**

**Your client asks you to connect to their procurement department's Azure Analysis Service. You call up their data analyst, and he asks you what you need for the connection. What do you need to make the connection and what type of query connection can you use? Select the THREE correct responses.**

    A. Connection Requirement: Server name, e.g. asazure://westcentralus.asazure.windows.net/abc

    B. Connection Requirement: Admin name

    C. Connection Option: Import

D. Connection Option: Dual

E. Connection Option: Direct Query

F. Connection Option: Connect live

## Question 24:

You are a BI analyst for a digital marketing company. You have built a complex report that requires many custom DAX measures and tables. After releasing your report, senior management complains that it takes too long to load some key visuals. How would you identify the cause of the poorly performing report elements?

A. Use the Dataverse button to drill into likely performance issues

B. Use the Performance Analyzer to examine report element performance

C. Use the cross report drillthrough feature to examine performance across the report

D. Run an R script to determine the performance issues in report elements

## Question 25:

You have a Premium workspace at your company and you want to use automatic page refresh. What are TWO key considerations to enable automatic page refresh?

A. Use must first disable sharing of your workspace

B. Your capacity administrator must enable the feature

C. Your interval must be greater than the minimum refresh interval

D. Refresh time in a premium capacity is rounded to the nearest 30 minutes

## Question 26:

A medical devices company has contracted you to investigate their transportation provider's performance. The company has a series of metrics they use to monitor the transportation provider's performance, including on-time pickup, on-time delivery, billing accuracy etc. You are asked to find potential factors that contribute to the transportation provider's performance. What sort of visualization can help?

A. Scatter chart

B. Q&A chart

C. Key influencers chart

D. Decomposition tree chart

## Question 27:

The board of your company would like to see a report on their mobiles. So you go ahead and optimize the report for mobile. For each of the following statements, select Yes if the statement is true. Otherwise, select No.

| Statement | Yes | No |
|---|---|---|
| In the mobile layout, you can double-click the visual in the visualization pane and the visual will be added to the canvas. | | |
| You cannot set the layering order of visuals on the mobile layout canvas. | | |
| If you've defined a background color for a report page, the mobile-optimized report will have the same background color. | | |

A. Yes / No / No
B. No / No / Yes
C. Yes / Yes / No
D. Yes / No / Yes


**Question 28:**
**You discover a quality data source on your company's Azure SQL database. You decide to connect using a direct query to the database. What two things are necessary to successfully connect?**
A. Specify the fully qualified server name when connecting
B. Ensure firewall rules for the database are configured to 'allow access to Azure services'
C. Select automatic schema change detection
D. Tiles are refreshed once per day, so you must configure the schedule refresh


**Question 29:**
**Your company buys out a transportation company. You find that the company has several tables for customer records, all with the same structure and headings. You need to combine these tables to form a new single table for a customer segmentation analysis prior to merging the data into the parent company's system. What transformation should you use?**
A. Merge queries
B. Append queries as new
C. Append queries
D. Merge queries as new


**Question 30:**
**You are asked by management to allow a consultant's custom Power BI visual. However, by default, management wants no custom visuals. How would you enable the**

consultant's visual while maintaining the default requirement in the most efficient manner?
- A. Temporarily disable the tenant setting for custom visualization
- B. Use Power BI Desktop .pbiviz files with the custom visual
- C. Add the custom visuals to the organizational store
- D. Build a separate Power BI service instance for the custom visual

## Question 31:
**What Text Analytics AI Insights are NOT available in Power BI.**
- A. Language Detection
- B. Sentiment Analysis
- C. Key Phrase Extraction
- D. Word Sense Disambiguation

## Question 32:
**You create a Power BI report for a software company that uses AI for transportation companies. The company has a sales team across several countries and you create row-level security (RLS) in the model. Sales managers are restricted to access the data from their own country.**
**In Power BI Desktop you create roles for each country e.g. USA, Canada, UK, France etc. You add a DAX expression for each role in the region table to filter the country. You then add an Azure Active Directory security group for the country to each role. A new user starts in France.**
**What do you need to do for the new user such that they can only see the sales data for France?**
- A. In Power BI Desktop, edit the DAX expression on the role for France
- B. In Power BI Service, change the Power BI workspace security and change the user's email address to 'contributor
- C. Add the user to the Azure Active Directory for France.
- D. In Power BI Service, use 'test as role' and use the email address of the new employee

## Question 33:
**You build a dashboard that has an important gauge visual for a furniture manufacturer. The head of manufacturing wants an alert whenever the gauge exceeds a certain value. What are the two options for configuring an alert in Power BI Service?**
- A. Use Microsoft Dataverse alert API
- B. Send an email
- C. Send a notification to mobile
- D. Use Microsoft Power Automate to trigger additional actions

## Question 34:
**What is NOT part of the Power BI Service dashboard theme?**
- A. Dark
- B. Light
- C. Color-blind friendly
- D. Custom
- E. Tab-order friendly


## Question 35:
**You decide to add a KPI visual for your company's dashboard. You need to show total units this year, show the historic values at a monthly level and for the comparison use total units last year. What fields should be used from the exhibit below in the KPI wells: Indicator, Trend Axis and Target Goals?**

| Table | Fields |
|-------|--------|
| Sales | Sales variance |
| | Sales variance % |
| | Total Units Last Year |
| | Total Units This Year |
| | Total Sales Value |
| Date | Fiscal Year |
| | Fiscal Month |
| | Fiscal Day |

- A. Indicator: Sales Units This Year, Trend axis: Fiscal Month, Target Goals: Sales Units This year
- B. Indicator: Sales Units This Year, Trend axis: Fiscal Month, Target Goals: Sales Units Last year
- C. Indicator: Sales Units Last Year, Trend axis: Fiscal Month, Target Goals: Sales Units This year
- D. Indicator: Sales Units This Year, Trend axis: Fiscal Year, Target Goals: Sales Units Last year


## Question 36:
**You import a customer table from a flat file into your data model. You have been asked to investigate the performance of your model and decide to check all the data sources 'view native query' . When you come to the customer table, you find that the 'view native query' does not display. What is a possible cause for 'view native query' being disabled?**
- A. Flat files do not support query folding
- B. In the transformation, there is a promoted headers step that blocks the native query
- C. You have used import as the storage mode

D. There is row-level security on the dataset

**Question 37:**
Please complete the below sentence.
If your dataset resides on a Premium capacity you can schedule up to _____ refreshes per day in the _____ settings. You can also trigger an _____ refresh by selecting Refresh now in the dataset menu.
  A. 24 / Power BI Desktop dataset / on-demand
  B. 16 / Power BI Service dataset / auto
  C. 8 / Power BI Service dataset / auto
  D. 48 / Power BI Service dataset / on-demand

**Question 38:**
You create a report for a hospital and use row-level security (RLS) for doctors to view their metrics and salary using a 'doctors' role. You also create a 'hospital manager' role that can see all the data. The employee table you use for RLS has id, name, role and email address. For each of the following statements, select Yes if the statement is true, otherwise select No.

| Statement | Yes | No |
|---|---|---|
| Doctors will be able to see their wages | | |
| Setting the DAX filter on the 'doctors' role to [email address] = USERPRINCIPALNAME() allows doctors to see only their metrics | | |
| Setting the DAX filter for hospital managers role to FALSE() allows hospital managers to view all the data | | |

  A. Yes / Yes / No
  B. Yes / Yes / Yes
  C. Yes / No / No
  D. No / Yes / No

**Question 39:**
You import the below Transport table into your model and have been instructed to find the totals across destination ZIP codes. Which summarization option would you recommend for aggregating the below three columns?
· DestinationZIP
· Weight
· Units

97

| Table Name | Column Name | Data Type |
|---|---|---|
| Transport | ConsignmentID | Whole Number |
| | ShipDate | Date |
| | PickupID | Whole Number |
| | DestinationID | Whole Number |
| | DestinationZIP | Text |
| | Weight | Decimal |
| | Units | Whole Number |

A. MAX / NONE / SUM
B. COUNT / SUM / NONE
C. NONE / SUM / SUM
D. NONE / MAX / SUM


**Question 40:**

You work as a BI engineer at an Oil and Gas company. You are asked to calculate a year to date calculation on the sales across your dataset. You have generated a date table using M code that has the date and year field. You also have a calculated measure called 'Sales Total' which is the sum of the sales amount. See the exhibit below for the desired output in the column 'Sales YTD'. What are two ways to calculate the year to date sales from your data?

| Year | Month Name | Sales Total | Sales YTD |
|---|---|---|---|
| 2017 | Jul | $1,423,357.32 | $1,423,357.32 |
| 2017 | Aug | $2,057,902.45 | $3,481,259.78 |
| 2017 | Sep | $2,523,947.55 | $6,005,207.32 |
| 2017 | Oct | $561,681.48 | $6,566,888.80 |
| 2017 | Nov | $4,764,920.16 | $11,331,808.96 |
| 2017 | Dec | $596,746.56 | $11,928,555.52 |
| 2018 | Jan | $1,327,674.63 | $1,327,674.63 |
| 2018 | Feb | $3,936,463.31 | $5,264,137.93 |
| 2018 | Mar | $700,873.18 | $5,965,011.12 |
| 2018 | Apr | $1,519,275.24 | $7,484,286.36 |
| 2018 | May | $2,960,378.09 | $10,444,664.45 |
| **Total** | | **$109,809,274.20** | |

| A. | CALCULATE ([Sales Total],<br>FILTER( |
|---|---|

| | |
|---|---|
| | ALL(Date'),<br>'Date' [Year] = MAX('Date' [Yea r]) &&<br>'Date'[Date]< = MAX('Date'[Date])<br>  )<br>) |
| B. | TOTALQTD([Sales Total],'Date'&[Date]) |
| C. | TOTALYTD([Sales Total],'Date'&[Date]) |
| D. | CALCULATE ([Sales Total],<br>FILTER(<br>'Date',<br>'Date [Year] = MAX( Dat&[Year]) &&<br>'Date' [Date]< = MAXÇDate[Date])<br>  )<br>) |

## Question 41:

Your manager at a construction materials company wants to know how category sales have changed over time with an animation. You decide that a chart with an animation to show changes across months would help visualize the data. How would you go about achieving this objective?

    A. Create a line chart and add month to the axis well

    B. Create a waterfall chart and add month to the breakdown well

    C. Create a scatter chart and add month to the play axis well

    D. Create a tree map and add month to the details well

## Question 42:

You are asked to create a measure to calculate the sales amount including the value added tax with the ability to go to the lowest level of detail (row level.) In addition, the value added tax is only relevant for order dates after Jan/1/2018. Prior to 2018, there is no tax applicable. See the exhibit below as an example of the output. How would you achieve this goal using a DAX expression?

| Year | Month Name | Sales Amount | Sales Tax | Conditional Sales With Tax |
|------|-----------|-------------|-----------|---------------------------|
| 2017 | Jul | $1,423,357.32 | $142,335.73 | $1,423,357.32 |
| 2017 | Aug | $2,057,902.45 | $205,790.25 | $2,057,902.45 |
| 2017 | Sep | $2,523,947.55 | $252,394.76 | $2,523,947.55 |
| 2017 | Oct | $561,681.48 | $56,168.15 | $561,681.48 |
| 2017 | Nov | $4,764,920.16 | $476,492.03 | $4,764,920.16 |
| 2017 | Dec | $596,746.56 | $59,674.66 | $596,746.56 |
| 2018 | Jan | $1,327,674.63 | $132,767.47 | $1,460,442.10 |
| 2018 | Feb | $3,936,463.31 | $393,646.34 | $4,330,109.65 |
| 2018 | Mar | $700,873.18 | $70,087.32 | $770,960.50 |
| 2018 | Apr | $1,519,275.24 | $151,927.53 | $1,671,202.77 |
| 2018 | May | $2,960,378.09 | $296,037.82 | $3,256,415.91 |
| 2018 | Jun | $1,487,671.19 | $148,767.13 | $1,636,438.33 |
| 2018 | Jul | $2,939,691.00 | $293,969.12 | $3,233,660.11 |
| 2018 | Aug | $3,964,801.20 | $396,480.14 | $4,361,281.35 |
| 2018 | Sep | $3,287,605.93 | $328,760.61 | $3,616,366.54 |
| **Total** | | **$109,809,274.20** | **$10,980,927.69** | **$119,597,346.32** |

A. SUM(sales[Sales Amount]) + SUM(sales[Sales Tax])

B. SUMX(sales,if(sales[OrderDate]> = DATE(2018,1,1 ),sales[Sales Amount]+sales[Sales Tax],sales[Sales Amount]))

C. SUMX(filter(sales,sales[OrderDate] > =DATE(2018,1,1)),sales[Sales Amount]+sales[Sales Tax])

D. SUM(sales,if(sales[OrderDate]> ='1/1/2018',sales[Sales Amount] +sales[Sales Tax],sales[Sales Amount]))

## Question 43:

At your company, you are the Power BI administrator. Your company policy states that only DA-100 certified people are allowed to create new workspaces. The people who are DA-100 certified are grouped into a security group called DA100Workspace. You hire several new people who have recently completed their DA-100 certification and assign them to the DA100Workspace security group.

The new users complain that they cannot create new workspaces. What three actions do you need to take in sequence in the admin portal to fix this issue?

Possible actions:

I. Navigate to Power BI admin portal and select Tenant settings

II. Navigate to office 365 admin security and select settings

III. Choose specific security groups to apply to and add DA100Workspace

IV. Click on Workspace settings and then click on create workspaces

V. Click refresh

A. i / iv / iii
B. ii / iii / v
C. ii / iv / v

D. i / ii / iii

## Question 44:

You have built a dashboard for the board of a soft drink company. One of the board members has some ideas he wants to test with several visuals from a report page. However, he wants to be able to immediately see the updates in the dashboard after you make changes. How would you go about doing this in the most efficient manner?

A. Create a new dashboard for every new request and pin the new tiles
B. Pin the report page as live to the dashboard
C. On the report page, select embed in dashboard
D. Create a hyperlink for the tiles and select embed in dashboard

## Question 45:

You work for a rapid fashion company and are tasked with calculating the percentage change in sales from last month. You are given a measure Sales Total that aggregates sales and you have a date table you built in DAX. How would you calculate last month's sales percentage change?

| A. | VAR SalesLastMonth = CALCULATE([Sales Total],DATEADDCDat& [Date], -1, MONTH)) <br> VAR SalesPercentageChange = DIVIDE([Sales Total]-SalesLastMonth,SalesLastMonth) <br> Return SalesPercentageChange |
|---|---|
| B. | VAR SalesLastMonth = CALCULATE9[Sales Total], PARALLELPERIOD ('Date'[Date],=1,QUARTER)) <br> VAR SalesPercentageChange = DIVIDE([Sales Total]-SalesLastMonth,SalesLastMonth) <br> Return SalesPercentageChange |
| C. | VAR SalesLastMonth = CALCULATE([Sales Total], SAMEPERIODLASTYEAR (Date[Date])) <br> VAR SalesPercentageChange = DIVIDE([Sales Total]-SalesLastMonth,SalesLastMonth) <br> Return SalesPercentageChange |
| D. | VAR SalesLastMonth = CALCULATE([Sales Total], DATEADD('Date'[Date],-1,MONTH)) <br> VAR SalesPercentageChange = Sales Total-SalesLastMonth <br> Return SalesPercentageChange |

## Question 46:

Senior management wants you to add data classifications to your dashboards to raise awareness with those viewing your dashboards about what level of security should be used. For each of the following statements, select Yes if the statement is true. Otherwise, select No.

| Statement | Yes | No |
|---|---|---|
| If data classification is turned on, all dashboards start out with a default classification type. | | |
| If you turn data classification off, all of the tags are remembered. | | |
| Each classification has a name, a shorthand tag and an optional URL. | | |

A. Yes / Yes / Yes
B. No / Yes / No
C. No / No / Yes
D. Yes / No / Yes


Question 47:
You have created a measure for the percentage of sales subcategory to sales and wish to apply conditional formatting as per the below exhibit. The rule you want to use is if the value is less than 10%, then shade the cell blue and if the value is greater than 10%, then shade the cell green. How would you complete the below conditional formatting table?

| Category | Sales Total | Sales % Category |
|---|---|---|
| ⊟ Accessories | $1,272,057.89 | 100.0% |
| Helmets | $484,048.53 | 38.1% |
| Tires and Tubes | $246,454.53 | 19.4% |
| Bike Racks | $237,096.16 | 18.6% |
| Hydration Packs | $105,826.42 | 8.3% |
| Bottles and Cages | $64,274.79 | 5.1% |
| Fenders | $46,619.58 | 3.7% |
| Bike Stands | $39,591.00 | 3.1% |
| Cleaners | $18,406.97 | 1.4% |
| Locks | $16,225.22 | 1.3% |
| Pumps | $13,514.69 | 1.1% |
| ⊞ Bikes | $94,620,526.21 | 100.0% |
| ⊞ Clothing | $2,117,613.45 | 100.0% |
| ⊞ Components | $11,799,076.66 | 100.0% |
| Total | $109,809,274.20 | 100.0% |

Background color - *Sales % Category*

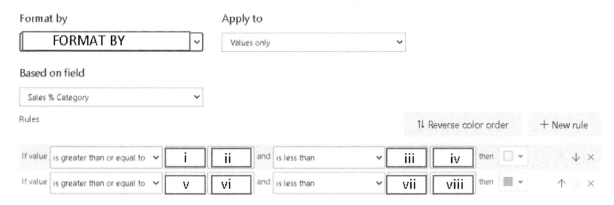

A. Format: 'Color Scale', Row 1: '0/ Number' and '10 / Number', Row 2: '10 / Number' and '100/ Number'
B. Format: 'Field Value', Row 1: '0/ Percentage' and '10/ Percentage', Row 2: '10 / Percentage' and '100 / Percentage'
C. Format: 'Rules', Row 1: '0/ Number' and '0.1 / Number', Row 2: '0.1 / Number' and '1 / Number
D. Format: 'Color Scale, Row 1: '0 / Percentage' and '10 / Percentage', Row 2: '10 / Percentage' and '100/ Percentage'

## Question 48:
**You work for a winemaker who has a selection of white and red wines that are fermented in barrels. The process can take between 5 and 35 months. Your data set has columns for fermentation time, start and end date. You need to create a bar chart that shows wine fermentation time in ranges of 5 months. When creating the bar chart, which four actions should you perform in sequence?**
   A. Select the fermentation time column, right click and select New Group -> Set Group type to Bin -> Set the Bin type to number of bins -> Make the bin count 6
   B. Set Group type to list -> Select the fermentation time column, right click and select New Group -> Set the Bin type to number of bins -> Make the bin count 30
   C. Select the fermentation time column, right click and select New Group -> Set the Bin type to count of bins -> Set Group type to Bin -> Make the bin size 6
   D. Select the fermentation time column, right click and select New Group -> Set Group type to Bin -> Make the bin count 30 -> Set the Bin type to number of bins

## Question 49:
**Your company has a current year target of last year's sales multiplied by an additional 10%. You have a date table called 'date' and you have a measure to sum sales called 'Sales Total.' How would you go about creating a DAX measure to calculate this?**

| | |
|---|---|
| A. | VAR PreviousYearSales = SUMX([Sales Total], SAMEPERIODLASTYEAR ('Date'[Date], -1, YEAR))<br>VAR TargetSales = PreviousYearSales*1.1<br>Return TargetSales |
| B. | VAR PreviousYearSales = CALCULATE([Sales Total], DATEADD('Date'[Date], -1,YEAR))<br>VAR TargetSales = PreviousYearSales*1.1<br>Return TargetSales |
| C. | VAR PreviousYearSales = CALCULATETABLE([Sales Total], DATEADD('Date'[Date], -1,YEAR))<br>VAR TargetSales = PreviousYearSales*1.1<br>Return TargetSales |
| D. | VAR PreviousYearSales = CALCULATE([Sales Total], PARALLELPERIOD ('Date'[Date], -1,MONTH))<br>VAR TargetSales = PreviousYearSales*1.1<br>Return PreviousYearSales |

**Question 50:**
You work for a cryptocurrency exchange as a BI analyst. You are tasked with creating a report for weekly trends across the asset ranges. Your source dataset has over 150 million rows. What two things can you do to optimize the report performance?
   A. Use the Direct Query storage mode for the dataset
   B. Only use line charts for visuals
   C. Use the Import storage mode for the dataset
   D. Do not use tab or layer order
   E. Create a summary table in the source data grouped by weekly volumes

**Question 51:**
You work for a bicycle manufacturer and you have created a bar chart with sales by category. Your boss wants to know the median sales, the 50th percentile of values in a column, rather than the total sales for each category. What are the two ways to achieve this goal?
   A. Create a new measure using the MEDIAN DAX function on the sales column
   B. In the analytics pane, add a trendline
   C. In the chart values well, right click on sales and change the summarization to Median
   D. Create a new measure using the Count (distinct) DAX function on the sales column
   E. In the chart values well, right click on sales and change the show value as to a percent of grand total

**Question 52:**

Your users give you feedback that they would like your reports to have more interactivity. You add some interactivity. To answer, select the following feature for each requirement from top to bottom. A feature may be used once, more than once, or not at all.

Features:
- Back button
- Tab selection
- Bookmarks
- Edit interactions
- Format pane

| Requirement | Answer |
|---|---|
| Edit the way visuals within the same page respond when a data point is selected. | |
| Create a view of a report with specific filters applied. | |
| A way for users to return to the previous page. | |

A. Tab selection / Format pane / Back button
B. Edit interactions / Bookmarks / Back button
C. Edit interactions / Tab selection / Back button
D. Bookmarks / Edit interactions / Back button


Question 53:
You find that your visuals on a report page are taking a long time to load and you need to find the cause. You remember there is a way to get how each of your report elements, such as visuals and DAX formulas, are performing. What five actions should you take in sequence from the below set of potential steps.
- Open performance analyzer and press start recording
- Ineract with the visuals
- Restart Power BI
- Press stop and review results
- Open query diagnostics and press start recording
- Click on SQL Server diagnostics
- Check enable diagnostics logging
- Create a blank report page

A. Restart Power BI -> Open performance analyzer and press start recording -> Check enable diagnostics logging -> Press stop and review results
B. Create a blank report page -> Restart Power BI -> Click on SQL Server diagnostics-> Ineract with the visuals -> Press stop and review results
C. Create a blank report page -> Restart Power BI -> Open performance analyzer and press start recording -> Ineract with the visuals -> Press stop and review results
D. Restart Power BI -> Open query diagnostics and press start recording -> Ineract with the visuals -> Press stop and review results

**Question 54:**

**You have a dataset in Power BI Service, and you want to use Quick Insights to get some ideas for a dashboard. However, you notice that Quick Insights are not working. What are the three possible reasons why Quick Insights is not working?**

A. You have uploaded data to Power BI
B. Your dataset uses Direct Query
C. Your dataset uses streaming
D. You have measures in your dataset
E. Your dataset is not statistically significant

**Question 55:**

**You have two visuals as per the below exhibit. You have the sales by year on the left, and on the right, you have sales by category. You need to configure the visual interaction between the two charts.**

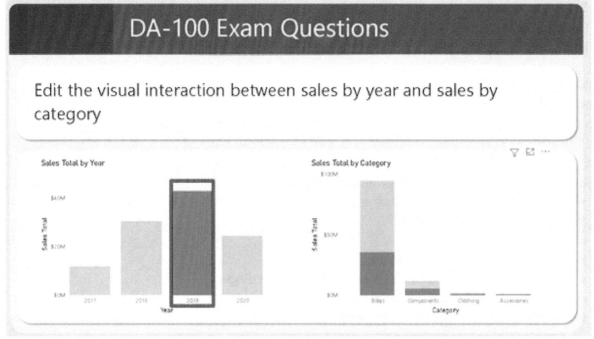

**For each of the following statements, select Yes if the statement is true. Otherwise, select No.**

| Statement | Yes | No |
|---|---|---|
| If you do not want the sales by year chart to filter the sales by category chart, set the interaction behaviour to None. | | |
| If you want the sales by year chart to highlight the sales by category chart, select the sales by category chart and edit the interaction on the sales by year chart. | | |
| To focus on the proportion of sales by category for a selected year, you should set the interaction behaviour to Filter. | | |

    A. Yes / No / Yes
    B. Yes / No / No
    C. No / No / Yes
    D. Yes / Yes / No


**Question 56:**
**Your company has a Power BI Premium license and you want to use the AI features in your report to expose insights. Which of the following two statements is NOT true?**
    A. You can take a piece of text and return a list of key phrases
    B. You can build your own machine learning models and use them in Power BI desktop
    C. The decomposition tree requires a premium subscription
    D. Sentiment Analysis is available for select languages
    E. You cannot use Power BI to tag images

# 4.1 Mock Test 2 Answer Sheet

**Question 1:**
**CASE 1**
**You work as a BI analyst for a software company that allows users to manipulate images online. You have built a report that shows the conversion from free customers to premium customers. Your boss has asked you to provide a filter for the 'marketing' industry.**
**Solution:**
- **Apply a filter on all pages of the report for the 'marketing' industry**
- **Share the report**
- **Mark share report with current filters and slicer options**

**Does this solution meet the requirements?**

   A. Yes
   B. No.

**Answer: A.**

Explanation
The answer is A.
The solution does meet the requirements for your boss. Since you have shared the report with current filters and slicers, you can share the filtered version of the report. Note that the end-user will have access to the dataset and can query other industries as well. To prevent the user from seeing other industries, you need to implement Row Level Security (RLS).

**Question 2:**
**CASE 1**
**You work as a BI analyst for a software company that allows users to manipulate images online. You have built a report that shows the conversion from free customers to premium customers. Your boss has asked you to provide a filter for the 'marketing' industry.**
**Solution:**
- **Create a text parameter for industry**
- **Set the parameter equal to 'marketing'**
- **Create a query parameter on the industry column**

**Does this solution meet the requirements?**

   A. Yes
   B. No.

**Answer: A.**

Explanation

The solution is A.

The method does meet the goal. Go to Power Query Editor and create the parameter and apply it to the industry column. The report will filter the data to customers in the 'marketing' industry.

## Question 3:
**CASE 1**

**You work as a BI analyst for a software company that allows users to manipulate images online. You have built a report that shows the conversion from free customers to premium customers. Your boss has asked you to provide a filter for the 'marketing' industry.**

**Solution:**
- **Add a slicer to the report and select the 'marketing' industry**
- **Sync slicers to all relevant pages of the report**

**Does this solution meet the requirements?**

A. Yes
B. No

**Answer: A.**

Explanation
The solution is A.

The method does meet the goal. A slicer is another method to filter the data. Syncing the slicer across all relevant pages to the industry ensures that the filter applies to all visuals. Note that the end-user will have access to the dataset and can query other industries as

## Question 4:
**CASE 2**

**You work for a financial institution, and you have built a data model and report in Power BI desktop. The report ran fine during testing, but when in production, users are complaining of performance issues. How can you improve the model's performance?**

**Solution: Hide intermediate tables in the model view**

**Does this help improve performance?**

A. Yes
B. No

**Answer: B.**

Explanation
The answer is B. Hiding intermediate tables does not affect the performance of the model. Hiding tables can help to clean up the model and create a better user experience, but it does not help to reduce the model size and there is no effect on performance.

## Question 5:

**CASE 2**

**You work for a financial institution, and you have built a data model and report in Power BI desktop. The report ran fine during testing, but when in production, users are complaining of performance issues. How can you improve the model's performance?**

**Solution: Convert source PO text column into a number by removing prefix, e.g. 'PO12399' to 12399**

**Does this help improve performance?**

    A. Yes

    B. No.

**Answer: A.**

Explanation

The answer is A. Removing the PO prefix and converting the column to a whole number reduces the model size and increases performance. For large tables, it can result in significant data reduction, especially when the column contains unique or high cardinality values.

**Question 6:**

**CASE 2**

**You work for a financial institution, and you have built a data model and report in Power BI desktop. The report ran fine during testing, but when in production, users are complaining of performance issues. How can you improve the model's performance?**

**Solution: Remove unnecessary columns**

**Does this help improve performance?**

    A. Yes

    B. No

**Answer: A.**

Explanation

The answer is A. Removing unnecessary columns reduces the model size and increases performance.

**Question 7:**

**CASE 3**

**You have the schema for the tables used in a bicycle franchise. In your role as a BI consultant, you have been asked to generate some insights from the data.**

**Company data schema:**

| Table Name | Column Name | Data Type |
|---|---|---|
| Sales | CustomerKey | Whole number |
| | Order Quantity | Fixed decimal |
| | OrderDate | Date |
| | OrderDateKey | Whole number |
| | ProductKey | Whole number |
| | Sales Amount | Fixed decimal |
| | SalesOrderLineKey | Whole number |
| | SalesTerritoryKey | Whole number |
| | UnitPrice | Fixed decimal |
| Sales orders | Channel | Text |
| | Sales Order | Text |
| | Sales Order Line | Text |
| | SalesOrderLineKey | Whole number |
| Product | Category | Text |
| | Color | Text |
| | ListPrice | Fixed decimal |
| | Model | Text |
| | Product | Text |
| | ProductKey | Text |
| | SKU | Text |
| | Standard Cost | Fixed decimal |
| | Subcategory | Text |
| Date | Date | Date |
| | Day Number | Whole number |
| | Month Number | Whole number |
| | Year | Whole number |
| Customer | CustomerKey | Text |
| | Name | Text |
| | Post Code | Whole number |

**You are asked to create a visualization for the sales by product. However, what should you do before creating a relationship?**

    A. Change the datatype of Sales[ProductKey] to fixed decimal

    B. Create a calculated column of Product[ProductKey]

    C. Change the datatype of Product[ProductKey] to whole number

    D. Create a measure for the sum of Sales[Order Quantity]

**Answer: C.**

Explanation

The answer is C.

The key in the sales table Sales[ProductKey] is of type whole number. For a relationship to work, the fields must be of the same data type. Hence, you should change the datatype of Product[ProductKey] to a whole number.

You should not change the datatype of Sales[ProductKey] to fixed decimal as this does not help the relationship in the Product table.

You should not create a calculated column of Product[ProductKey] as this will not help the relationship between Sales[ProductKey] and Product[ProductKey].

A measure for Sales[Order Quantity] is not helpful in creating a relationship between tables.

**Question 8:**
**CASE 3**
**You have the schema for the tables used in a bicycle franchise. In your role as a BI consultant, you have been asked to generate some insights from the data.**
**Company data schema:**

| Table Name | Column Name | Data Type |
|---|---|---|
| Sales | CustomerKey | Whole number |
| | Order Quantity | Fixed decimal |
| | OrderDate | Date |
| | OrderDateKey | Whole number |
| | ProductKey | Whole number |
| | Sales Amount | Fixed decimal |
| | SalesOrderLineKey | Whole number |
| | SalesTerritoryKey | Whole number |
| | UnitPrice | Fixed decimal |
| Sales orders | Channel | Text |
| | Sales Order | Text |
| | Sales Order Line | Text |
| | SalesOrderLineKey | Whole number |
| Product | Category | Text |
| | Color | Text |
| | ListPrice | Fixed decimal |
| | Model | Text |
| | Product | Text |
| | ProductKey | Text |
| | SKU | Text |
| | Standard Cost | Fixed decimal |

| | Subcategory | Text |
|---|---|---|
| Date | Date | Date |
| | Day Number | Whole number |
| | Month Number | Whole number |
| | Year | Whole number |
| Customer | CustomerKey | Text |
| | Name | Text |
| | Post Code | Whole number |

**The product table's color column has abbreviations as well as names. For instance, there is both Black and BLK. What do you need to do to ensure consistency in the color column?**

A. Export the table to Excel
B. Use replace values in the transform ribbon in Power Query Editor
C. Edit the source applied step in M code
D. Remove duplicates in Power Query Editor

**Answer: B.**

Explanation
The answer is B.
You should use replace values in Power Query Editor to ensure the color names are consistent. For instance you would replace 'BLK' with 'Black'. You should not export the table to Excel as this will not fix the data inconsistency in the colors column. You should not edit the source applied step in M code as this only tells Power BI where your source data is located. Do not use the remove duplicates transformation as this will delete rows from your table.

**Question 9:**
**CASE 3**
**You have the schema for the tables used in a bicycle franchise. In your role as a BI consultant, you have been asked to generate some insights from the data.**
**Company data schema:**

| Table Name | Column Name | Data Type |
|---|---|---|
| Sales | CustomerKey | Whole number |
| | Order Quantity | Fixed decimal |
| | OrderDate | Date |
| | OrderDateKey | Whole number |
| | ProductKey | Whole number |
| | Sales Amount | Fixed decimal |

| | SalesOrderLineKey | Whole number |
|---|---|---|
| | SalesTerritoryKey | Whole number |
| | UnitPrice | Fixed decimal |
| Sales orders | Channel | Text |
| | Sales Order | Text |
| | Sales Order Line | Text |
| | SalesOrderLineKey | Whole number |
| Product | Category | Text |
| | Color | Text |
| | ListPrice | Fixed decimal |
| | Model | Text |
| | Product | Text |
| | ProductKey | Text |
| | SKU | Text |
| | Standard Cost | Fixed decimal |
| | Subcategory | Text |
| Date | Date | Date |
| | Day Number | Whole number |
| | Month Number | Whole number |
| | Year | Whole number |
| Customer | CustomerKey | Text |
| | Name | Text |
| | Post Code | Whole number |

**When reviewing the customer table, you find that some of the postcodes appear to be missing. For instance '0800' does not seem to exist. What do you need to do to ensure all the Postcodes from the original data are in your model?**

A. Use 'add columns from examples' to fix discrepancies

B. Use 'transform' and then adjust the rounding

C. Go to the transform ribbon and click on 'Use first row as header'

D. Make sure the postcode data type is 'text' and not 'whole number'

**Answer: D.**

Explanation

The answer is D. If the original data uses '0' as a prefix for some post codes, converting to a whole number will remove the zero. For instance '0800' becomes 800. To prevent losing this data, change the postcode data type to 'text' in the applied step 'Changed Type.' Note that column profiling is based on the first 1000 rows and if Power BI does not see any cases of zero prefixes, the tool will assume the column is a whole number.

You should not use the add columns from examples as the issue is in the data type conversion.

You should not adjust the rounding of the postcode number. The problem is at the start of the number and not the end of the number. Using the first row as header addresses the column name and not the data type.

**Question 10:**
**CASE 3**
**You have the schema for the tables used in a bicycle franchise. In your role as a BI consultant, you have been asked to generate some insights from the data.**
**Company data schema:**

| Table Name | Column Name | Data Type |
|---|---|---|
| Sales | CustomerKey | Whole number |
| | Order Quantity | Fixed decimal |
| | OrderDate | Date |
| | OrderDateKey | Whole number |
| | ProductKey | Whole number |
| | Sales Amount | Fixed decimal |
| | SalesOrderLineKey | Whole number |
| | SalesTerritoryKey | Whole number |
| | UnitPrice | Fixed decimal |
| Sales orders | Channel | Text |
| | Sales Order | Text |
| | Sales Order Line | Text |
| | SalesOrderLineKey | Whole number |
| Product | Category | Text |
| | Color | Text |
| | ListPrice | Fixed decimal |
| | Model | Text |
| | Product | Text |
| | ProductKey | Text |
| | SKU | Text |
| | Standard Cost | Fixed decimal |
| | Subcategory | Text |

| Date | Date | Date |
|---|---|---|
| | Day Number | Whole number |
| | Month Number | Whole number |
| | Year | Whole number |
| Customer | CustomerKey | Text |
| | Name | Text |
| | Post Code | Whole number |

**You have been asked to add a column for profit, revenue – price. What steps do you need to do to calculate profit in the model?**

    A. Unpivot the Unit Price column -> Create custom column named Profit -> Set formula Sales Amount — (Order Quantity UnitPrice)

    B. Create custom column named Profit -> Set formula Sales Amount —(Order Quantity * UnitPrice) -> Set the data type to Fixed decimal

    C. Duplicate the Order Quantity Column -> Create a new column and multiply duplicated column by UnitPrice-> Create custom column named Profit

    D. Create a Group By on SalesOrderLineKey -> Sum by Sales Amount and rename Profit -> Subtract Unit Price

**Answer: B.**

Explanation

The answer is B.

You should perform the steps in the following order:

    1. Create custom column named Profit
    2. Set formula Sales Amount – (Order Quantity * UnitPrice)
    3. Set the data type to Fixed decimal

You should not unpivot the UnitPrice column. Unpivoting converts the data headers stored horizontally into a vertical format. This does not help you calculate profit.

Duplicating the Order Quantity column is an unnecessary additional step. You should not create a group by. A group by function is used to summarize rows and not used for row level calculations.

**Question 11:**

**You have some new staff joining your Power BI team. To help them get started in Power BI Desktop, you want to create a way for them to connect to the data sources that you are using in your project. All they will need to do to connect to the data is enter their user credentials to authenticate. How can you achieve this?**

    A. Create a dynamic M query
    B. Use an Excel Macro to build connections
    C. Create a PBIDS file with your key data sources
    D. Create a template in lineage view

116

**Answer: C.**

Explanation
The answer is C. You can create a PBIDS file to streamline the experience for new or beginner report creators in your organization. If you create the PBIDS file from existing reports, it's easier for beginning report authors to build new reports from the same data.
In answer A, a dynamic M query does not assist in enabling data source connections.
In answer B, an Excel Macro cannot be used to create a template for a Power BI report
In answer C, you cannot create a data template in the lineage view in Power BI Service.

**Question 12:**
**You use an R script to build a custom visual. However, you find that you cannot see data marked 'N/A' and you are getting an error when importing your data as a list. What could be TWO reasons for these issues?**
   A. 'NA' is transformed into 'NULL' by Power BI
   B. You have not used the correct R version
   C. Power BI only supports R dataframes
   D. You need to first install the library 'tidyr'

**Answer: A, C.**

Explanation
The answer is A and C. Values that are N/A in your data are translated to NULL values in Power BI Desktop. Only data frames are imported into Power BI, so be sure to represent the data you want to import in a data frame. Power BI does not support lists, matrices and other data structures
Answer B is incorrect, the version of R will not influence these issues.
Answer D is incorrect. The 'tidyr' library is not required, it is used for changing the layout of your data sets.

**Question 13:**
**You have an inactive relationship between your date table and your shipping table. How would you use an inactive relationship in a measure?**
   A. Use the LOOKUPVALUE() function
   B. Delete the active relationship and make the new relationship active
   C. Use the USERELATIONSHIP() function
   D. Change the crossfilter direction to both in the modeling tab

**Answer: C.**

Explanation
The answer is C. The USERELATIONSHIP() function specifies an existing relationship to be used in the evaluation of a DAX expression. Do not use the LOOKUPVALUE() function. The

LOOKUPVALUE() retrieves a value from a table, but we need to connect a relationship for the measure. Do not delete an active relationship as this will break any existing visuals created. Do not change the crossfilter direction. The crossfilter direction is used to allow the data to be filtered in either direction.

**Question 14:**
**Your client has asked you whether you can create data alerts for all of the key visuals on your dashboard. Which two visuals can you NOT create a data alert for?**
    A. Funnel chart
    B. KPI chart
    C. Stacked column chart
    D. Gauge chart

**Answer: A, C.**

Explanation
The correct options are Funnel chart and Stacked column chart.
Data alerts are a feature in Power BI that allows you to set notifications when data on a dashboard changes beyond the limits you set. Data alerts can only be set on tiles pinned from report visuals, and only on gauges, KPIs, and cards. Data alerts are not supported for other types of visuals, such as funnel charts or stacked column charts.

The other options are incorrect because:
• KPI chart: This is a type of visual that can have data alerts set on it. A KPI chart displays a key performance indicator (KPI) along with a trend line or a variance to a target value. You can set data alerts on a KPI chart to monitor the progress or performance of a metric that is important to your business or organization.
• Gauge chart: This is another type of visual that can have data alerts set on it. A gauge chart displays a single value within a range of values, along with a needle that indicates where the value falls within the range. You can set data alerts on a gauge chart to track the status or level of a measure that has a defined minimum and maximum value.

**Question 15:**
**You build a key influencer visual and you want to see how sales amount is affected by product category and product color. How do you complete the three fields below?**

118

Visualizations

Analyze

Add data fields here

Explain by

Add data fields here

Expand by

Add data fields here

A. Analyze -> Sales[Sales Quantity]; Explain by -> Product[Category], Product[Color]
B. Analyze -> Sales[Sales Amount]; Expand by -> Product[Category], Product[Model]
C. Analyze -> Sales[Sales Quantity]; Explain by -> Product[Category]; Expand by -
   >Product[Color]
D. Analyze -> Sales[Sales Amount]; Explain by -> Product[Category], Product[Color]

**Answer: D.**

Explanation
The answer is D. As we want to analyze the sales amount, use Sales[Sales Amount] in the analysis well. We want to use product category and color, so add Product[Category] and Product[Color] to the explanation as well. Do not use Sales[Sales Quantity] as we were asked about sales amount. Do not use expand by. The expand by well is used when analyzing a measure or summarized field.

**Question 16:**
**You work for NASA's Supply Chain division. NASA purchases parts for the international space station. There are two key tables: SpaceStationInventory and DateTable. The SpaceStationInventory table contains the inventory counts for the parts and the date of the counts. The DateTable is a date table you created using M code. The Supply Chain division works Monday to Friday and is closed on state and federal holidays. As senior BI specialist you have been tasked to show the inventory level for the international space station warehouse on the last day of each month. Which DAX function will meet your requirement?**
   A. CALCULATE( SUM(SpaceStationInventory[Inventory Count]),
      LASTDATE(DateTable[Date])

B. CLOSINGBALANCEMONTH(SUMX(SpaceStationInventory[Inventory Count]),
   SpaceStationInventory[Date])
C. CALCULATE(SUM(SpaceStation Inventory[Inventory Count]),
   LASTDATE(SpaceStationInventory[Date])
D. CALCULATE(SUM(SpaceStation Inventory[Inventory Count]),
   FILTER(SpaceStationInventory, SpaceStationInventory[Inventory Count] =
   MAX(SpaceStationInventory[Inventory Count]))

**Answer: C.**

Explanation
The answer is C. The LASTDATE DAX function returns the last non blank date. We want the inventory count for the last date from the SpaceStationInventory table. You should not use LASTDATE on the date table. The date table has every date on the calendar including weekends and holidays. If the last date of the month is a non working day, we will get a zero inventory count.
Do not use the CLOSINGBALANCEMONTH DAX function. The function will show inventory for the final calendar date of the month. If the last date of the month is a non working day, we will get a zero inventory count.
If you filter by the MAX inventory count, you will get the peak during the month and not the ending inventory at the end of the month.

**Question 17:**
**You work for an electric car manufacturer and you need to import a Supplier table into your data model. The Supplier table lists the supplier id, full name, short name and address. When reviewing the data in Power BI, you want to check the distinct and unique rows for each column.**
   A. Column profile
   B. Monospaced
   C. Column distribution
   D. Show whitespace
   E. Column quality

**Answer: C.**

Explanation
The answer is C. The column distribution option shows the count of distinct and unique rows for each column. The column profile option shows a value distribution along with some statistical summary figures. The column quality shows the percentage of Valid, Error and Empty rows. The monospaced option sets all the data's preview font to monospaced. The show whitespaces option displays whitespace and newline characters.

**Question 18:**

You work for a large multinational company that has 23 departments. You have been tasked with creating a report with all the first aid trained staff . You need to create the same report for each department. How can you create the same report for each department in the most efficient manner?

A. Create separate Power BI Desktop report for each department and email the PBIX
B. Add a parameter to the report to filter department
C. Create a separate workspace for each department and create a report in each
D. Create a separate dataset for each department and add a separate report

**Answer: B.**

Explanation

The answer is B. You can add a parameter on the report to filter the department. This allows you to use the same report across all departments. You should not create separate Power BI Desktop files as this is an inefficient and time consuming way to distribute 23 reports.
You should not create separate workspaces for each department as this duplicates the report and is time consuming. Workspaces are used for collaboration and there is no need for separate collaboration for every department. You should not create a separate dataset for each department as this also duplicates the report and is time consuming.

**Question 19:**
**You have produced reports for a space tourism startup. The founder is thrilled with the Power BI service setup. However, he has some questions on how to promote and secure the datasets to other users in the company. His three requirements are below:**

1. **When Power BI Service launches, I want the competition report to be displayed on their screen.**
2. **For the financial dashboard, I want the classification of the data clearly displayed.**
3. **I want you to highlight particular reports because it is valuable and worthwhile for others to use. I also don't want you to ask permission from the Power BI Admin each time.**

For the above requirements, them as either:
- **Certified**
- **Promoted**
- **Featured**
- **Sensitivity Label**

A. Promoted / Certified I Featured
B. Sensitivity Label / Featured / Promoted
C. Featured / Sensitivity Label / Promoted
D. Certified / Sensitivity Label / Promoted

**Answer: C.**

Explanation

The answer is C. When a report is marked as featured, it will appear on the Power BI home page.

To show data classification on a dashboard, you can use sensitivity labels. These labels appear next to the dashboard name. Sensitivity labels are created and managed in the Microsoft 365 compliance center.

Promotion and certification are types of endorsement. Promotion is a way to highlight the content you think is valuable and worthwhile for others to use. Promotion does not need any admin permissions. Certification means that the content meets the organization's quality standards and is regarded as reliable and ready for use across the organization. Certification does require admin permission.

## Question 20:

**You work for an electric scooter manufacturer. You have a report with five pages, and you have been asked to filter all five pages when you select a particular scooter category on the first page. What are the two ways you could do this?**
   A. Add a page level filter on all five pages
   B. Create a report level filter using category in the 'Filter all pages well
   C. Use a single button and set the action type to bookmark
   D. Select paginated report and configure the settings
   E. Create a slicer for category on each page and then Sync slicers on all pages

**Answer: B, E.**

Explanation
The answer is B and E.

A report level filter will create a filter on all five pages of the report. Similarly, if each page has a slicer for category, you can use 'sync slicers' to filter all pages together. A page filter will only apply to the one page and cannot be used to control all five pages at once. A single button cannot be used with a bookmark across multiple pages.

A paginated report is for creating 'pixel perfect' reports and is not used to filter reports across multiple pages.

## Question 21:

**A colleague built a Power BI desktop report. Your colleague imported a flat file into Power BI from his local machine. You have inherited the Power BI report and you need to update the source for the file. How would you go about this?**
   A. On the home ribbon, click on properties and change the file path
   B. Click on the Applied step 'source and click on the cog to change the file path
   C. On the home ribbon, click on manage -> then file, then change the file path
   D. Click on the Applied step 'changed type' and click on the cog in the corner to change the file location

**Answer: B.**

Explanation

The Answer is B.

You can adjust the source location of your file in Power Query Editor by clicking on the source applied step. In the right corner, click the cog and update the file path. The home ribbon properties button is used to change the name and description of the query and not the file location. The home ribbon manage button is used to delete, duplicate or reference a query. The manage button cannot be used to change a file's path.

**Question 22:**

**A colleague calls you for help. She wants to build an app in Power BI and asks you how to publish the app. What are the three most important parts of publishing an app? Select THREE from the below.**
   A. On the permissions tab, decide who has access to the app
   B. On the title tab, fill in the name and description to help people find the app
   C. Before releasing the app, create a digital signature, so people know who built the app
   D. On the navigation tab, select the content to be visible in the app
   E. Click the Sync to organization button
   F. On the setup tab, fill in the name and description to help people find the app

**Answer: A, D, F.**

Explanation

The answer is A, D and F.

When publishing an app, fill in the name and description in the setup tab to help people find your app. Next, under the navigation tab, select the content you want visible in the app. Finally, on the permissions tab, decide who has access to the app. You can select individual people or the entire organization.

There is no title tab when setting up an app. The only three tabs are set up, navigation and permission. You do not need to create a digital signature when releasing your app.

There is no Sync to organization button. There is only a publish app button at the bottom of the screen when you are done.

**Question 23:**

**Your client asks you to connect to their procurement department's Azure Analysis Service. You call up their data analyst, and he asks you what you need for the connection. What do you need to make the connection and what type of query connection can you use? Select the THREE correct responses.**
   A. Connection Requirement: Server name, e.g.
      asazure://westcentralus.asazure.windows.net/abc
   B. Connection Requirement: Admin name
   C. Connection Option: Import
   D. Connection Option: Dual
   E. Connection Option: Direct Query
   F. Connection Option: Connect live

**Answer: A, C, F.**

Explanation

The answer is A, C and F.

The steps to connection to the Azure Analysis Service are:

1. In Power BI Desktop, click Get Data > Azure > Azure Analysis Services database
2. Under Server, enter the server name. Include the full URL
   .g.asazure://westcentralus.asazure.windows.net/abc
3. Select a connection option. You can select either import or connect live

You do not need to submit an admin name when connecting to the Azure Analysis Service. The two connection options available are import and connect live. While you can use either, connect live is the recommended option as there are limitations to using the import option.

**Question 24:**

**You are a BI analyst for a digital marketing company. You have built a complex report that requires many custom DAX measures and tables. After releasing your report, senior management complains that it takes too long to load some key visuals. How would you identify the cause of the poorly performing report elements?**

    A. Use the Dataverse button to drill into likely performance issues

    B. Use the Performance Analyzer to examine report element performance

    C. Use the cross report drillthrough feature to examine performance across the report

    D. Run an R script to determine the performance issues in report elements

**Answer: B.**

Explanation

The answer is B.

In Power BI Desktop, you can find out how each of your report elements are performing. Using the Performance Analyzer, you can see and record logs that measure how your report elements perform. For example, DAX formulas and visuals performance timing when users interact with them. Dataverse lets you store and manage data that's used by business applications. The dataverse cannot be used for performance issues.

A drillthrough allows users to drillthrough on a visual to the focused page to get details that are filtered to that context. A drillthrough cannot be used for performance diagnostics.

**Question 25:**

**You have a Premium workspace at your company and you want to use automatic page refresh. What are TWO key considerations to enable automatic page refresh?**

    A. Use must first disable sharing of your workspace

    B. Your capacity administrator must enable the feature

    C. Your interval must be greater than the minimum refresh interval

    D. Refresh time in a premium capacity is rounded to the nearest 30 minutes

**Answer: B, C.**

Explanation
The answer is B and C.
You cannot use automatic data refresh unless your capacity administrator has enabled the feature. Secondly, the capacity administrator can set a minimum refresh interval. If your interval is less than the minimum refresh interval, the Power BI service overrides your interval to respect the minimum interval set by your capacity administrator.
You do not need to disable sharing of your workspace to set automatic page refresh. The refresh time is not rounded to the nearest 30 minutes.

**Question 26:**
**A medical devices company has contracted you to investigate their transportation provider's performance. The company has a series of metrics they use to monitor the transportation provider's performance, including on-time pickup, on-time delivery, billing accuracy etc. You are asked to find potential factors that contribute to the transportation provider's performance. What sort of visualization can help?**
- A. Scatter chart
- B. Q&A chart
- C. Key influencers chart
- D. Decomposition tree chart

**Answer: C.**

Explanation
The answer is C.
You should use a key influencers chart. A key influencers chart helps you understand the factors that drive a metric. You should not use a decomposition tree. A decomposition tree is an AI tool used for ad hoc exploration and conducting root cause analysis.
You should not use a scatter chart. A scatter chart is helpful to show outliers across a large data set. You should not use a Q&A visual. A Q&A visual helps users explore the data from questions using natural language algorithms.

**Question 27:**
**The board of your company would like to see a report on their mobiles. So you go ahead and optimize the report for mobile. For each of the following statements, select Yes if the statement is true. Otherwise, select No.**

| Statement | Yes | No |
|---|---|---|
| In the mobile layout, you can double-click the visual in the visualization pane and the visual will be added to the canvas. | | |
| You cannot set the layering order of visuals on the mobile layout canvas. | | |
| If you've defined a background color for a report page, the mobile-optimized report will have the same background color. | | |

    A. Yes / No / No
    B. No / No / Yes
    C. Yes / Yes / No
    D. Yes / No / Yes

**Answer: D.**

Explanation
The answer is D.
There are two ways to add a visual to a mobile layout. First, you can drag it from the Page visuals pane to the phone canvas. Alternatively, you can double-click the visual in the visualization pane.
You CAN set the layering order of visuals on the mobile layout canvas. The order of the list reflects the layer ordering on the canvas. Like a bird's eye view, the first listed visual is on the top-most layer, while the last listed visual is on the bottom-most layer.
A mobile-optimized report will follow the background color of the report page.

**Question 28:**
**You discover a quality data source on your company's Azure SQL database. You decide to connect using a direct query to the database. What two things are necessary to successfully connect?**
    A. Specify the fully qualified server name when connecting
    B. Ensure firewall rules for the database are configured to 'allow access to Azure services'
    C. Select automatic schema change detection
    D. Tiles are refreshed once per day, so you must configure the schedule refresh

**Answer: A, B.**

Explanation
The answer is A and B.
You must specify the full server name when connecting to the Azure SQL database. You can find your fully qualified server name and database name in the Azure portal. Make sure you

have configured the firewall rules to 'allow access to Azure service' or you may not be able to access your database. Schema changes are not automatically detected in Azure SQL database connections.

Tiles are refreshed once per hour by default. There is no requirement to configure a scheduled refresh. However, you can adjust how often to refresh in the Advanced settings when you connect.

**Question 29:**

**Your company buys out a transportation company. You find that the company has several tables for customer records, all with the same structure and headings. You need to combine these tables to form a new single table for a customer segmentation analysis prior to merging the data into the parent company's system. What transformation should you use?**

    A. Merge queries
    B. Append queries as new
    C. Append queries
    D. Merge queries as new

**Answer: B.**

Explanation
The answer is B.
The append query creates a single table by adding the contents of one or more tables to another, and aggregates the column headers from the tables to create the schema for the new table. An append query is similar to a Union query in SQL. Since the question asked for a new table, you should append the query as new.
You should not use the merge transformation. A merge transformation joins two existing tables together based on matching keys from one or multiple columns. This join is used to add columns to a data set and not used to add rows. A merge transformation is similar to a SQL join.

**Question 30:**

**You are asked by management to allow a consultant's custom Power BI visual. However, by default, management wants no custom visuals. How would you enable the consultant's visual while maintaining the default requirement in the most efficient manner?**

    A. Temporarily disable the tenant setting for custom visualization
    B. Use Power BI Desktop .pbiviz files with the custom visual
    C. Add the custom visuals to the organizational store
    D. Build a separate Power BI service instance for the custom visual

**Answer: C.**

Explanation
The answer is C.

Custom Power BI visuals created privately for your organization can be uploaded to the organizational store. Uploading the private files into your organizational store saves overhead and management time. The custom visuals are easily accessed by the Power BI users within the organization while still respecting the external restriction for custom visuals. Temporarily disabling the tenant settings is not an efficient way to manage your configuration.

While a local Power BI Desktop file could have custom visuals, when uploading to Power BI service, the custom visual would still be blocked. Building a separate instance of Power BI service is an expensive and inefficient solution to allow a single custom visual.

**Question 31:**
**What Text Analytics AI Insights are NOT available in Power BI.**
    A. Language Detection
    B. Sentiment Analysis
    C. Key Phrase Extraction
    D. Word Sense Disambiguation

**Answer: D.**

Explanation
The answer is D.
AI insights supports language detection, sentiment analysis and key phrase extraction. Word sense disambiguation involves detecting the meaning of a word within its context. For example, light can be used as a weight, a color or an electrical appliance. Word sense disambiguation is not available in Power BI.

**Question 32:**
**You create a Power BI report for a software company that uses AI for transportation companies. The company has a sales team across several countries and you create row-level security (RLS) in the model. Sales managers are restricted to access the data from their own country.**
**In Power BI Desktop you create roles for each country e.g. USA, Canada, UK, France etc. You add a DAX expression for each role in the region table to filter the country. You then add an Azure Active Directory security group for the country to each role. A new user starts in France.**
**What do you need to do for the new user such that they can only see the sales data for France?**
    A. In Power BI Desktop, edit the DAX expression on the role for France
    B. In Power BI Service, change the Power BI workspace security and change the user's email address to 'contributor
    C. Add the user to the Azure Active Directory for France.
    D. In Power BI Service, use 'test as role' and use the email address of the new employee

**Answer: C.**

Explanation

The answer is C.

You add the user to the Azure Active Directory for France. The row-level security groups have been configured to control the membership of each role. So, you should change their membership of Azure Active Directory security groups.

You should not edit the DAX expression on Power BI Desktop, this just defines the row filters for the role. Membership is controlled in Power BI service.

Do not add the new employee to the workspace as a contributor. The user will be able to see all the data and will not be restricted to the row level security settings.

Do not use the 'test as role' in Power BI Service. The 'test as role' is a way to preview the data for a role and is not used to assign roles to new members.

**Question 33:**

**You build a dashboard that has an important gauge visual for a furniture manufacturer. The head of manufacturing wants an alert whenever the gauge exceeds a certain value. What are the two options for configuring an alert in Power BI Service?**

    A. Use Microsoft Dataverse alert API

    B. Send an email

    C. Send a notification to mobile

    D. Use Microsoft Power Automate to trigger additional actions

**Answer: B, D.**

Explanation

The answer is B and D.

You can send an email or you can use Microsoft Power Automate to trigger an action. You can then use Power Automate to send a notification to Microsoft teams, text message, social media post or email. There is no Microsoft Dataverse alert API. Use Power Automate to listen for the alert trigger. Notifications of alerts are controlled by settings in the mobile app and cannot be configured in Power BI service.

**Question 34:**

**What is NOT part of the Power BI Service dashboard theme?**

    A. Dark

    B. Light

    C. Color-blind friendly

    D. Custom

    E. Tab-order friendly

**Answer: E.**

Explanation

The answer is E.

In Power BI Service you can adjust a dashboards theme to one of four options: Light, Dark, Color-blind friendly and custom JSON. Tab-order is created in a report under Selection > Tab order and is not a theme.

## Question 35:

**You decide to add a KPI visual for your company's dashboard. You need to show total units this year, show the historic values at a monthly level and for the comparison use total units last year. What fields should be used from the exhibit below in the KPI wells: Indicator, Trend Axis and Target Goals?**

| Table | Fields |
|---|---|
| Sales | Sales variance |
| | Sales variance % |
| | Total Units Last Year |
| | Total Units This Year |
| | Total Sales Value |
| Date | Fiscal Year |
| | Fiscal Month |
| | Fiscal Day |

A. Indicator: Sales Units This Year, Trend axis: Fiscal Month, Target Goals: Sales Units This year

B. Indicator: Sales Units This Year, Trend axis: Fiscal Month, Target Goals: Sales Units Last year

C. Indicator: Sales Units Last Year, Trend axis: Fiscal Month, Target Goals: Sales Units This year

D. Indicator: Sales Units This Year, Trend axis: Fiscal Year, Target Goals: Sales Units Last year

**Answer: B.**

Explanation
The answer is B.
The indicator is the measure to plot, so use Sales Units This Year. The trend axis is the period to show the data, so use Fiscal month. Lastly, the Target Goal is the field for comparison, so use Sales Units Last Year.

## Question 36:

**You import a customer table from a flat file into your data model. You have been asked to investigate the performance of your model and decide to check all the data sources 'view native query'. When you come to the customer table, you find that the 'view native query' does not display. What is a possible cause for 'view native query' being disabled?**

A. Flat files do not support query folding

B. In the transformation, there is a promoted headers step that blocks the native query
C. You have used import as the storage mode
D. There is row-level security on the dataset

**Answer: A.**

Explanation
The answer is A.
View native query relies on query folding, the ability to generate a single query statement to retrieve and transform source data. A flat file, we, blob and common data service do not allow query folding. Hence, view native query is disabled.
A promoted headers step is not relevant to whether query folding works or not. The import storage mode will still enable query folding for relational database sources. Lastly, row-level security is not relevant to the data source query folding.

**Question 37:**
**Please complete the below sentence.**
**If your dataset resides on a Premium capacity you can schedule up to _____ refreshes per day in the _____ settings. You can also trigger an _____ refresh by selecting Refresh now in the dataset menu.**
   A. 24 / Power BI Desktop dataset / on-demand
   B. 16 / Power BI Service dataset / auto
   C. 8 / Power BI Service dataset / auto
   D. 48 / Power BI Service dataset / on-demand

**Answer: D.**

Explanation
The answer is D.
You can configure up to eight daily time slots if your dataset is on shared capacity, or 48 time slots on Power BI Premium. Scheduled refreshes are set up in Power BI Service and you can trigger an on-demand refresh by selecting 'Refresh now' in the dataset menu.

**Question 38:**
**You create a report for a hospital and use row-level security (RLS) for doctors to view their metrics and salary using a 'doctors' role. You also create a 'hospital manager' role that can see all the data. The employee table you use for RLS has id, name, role and email address. For each of the following statements, select Yes if the statement is true, otherwise select No.**

| Statement | Yes | No |
|---|---|---|
| Doctors will be able to see their wages | | |
| Setting the DAX filter on the 'doctors' role to [email address] = USERPRINCIPALNAME() allows doctors to see only their metrics | | |
| Setting the DAX filter for hospital managers role to FALSE() allows hospital managers to view all the data | | |

A. Yes / Yes / No
B. Yes / Yes / Yes
C. Yes / No / No
D. No / Yes / No

**Answer: A.**

Explanation
The answer is A.
Since you applied row-level security to doctors, they will be able to see their wages and metrics. The DAX function USERPRINCIPALNAME(), returns the user's email address e.g. John.Smith@ABCHospital.com. When the DAX function sets the email address = USERPRINCIPALNAME(), we are using a dynamic row-level security method that will compare the user's email address to that in the employee table. This will then restrict the data that the doctor can see.
When the DAX filter for Hospital managers is set to TRUE(), the manager will see all the data. When the DAX filter is set to FALSE(), no data will be shown.

**Question 39:**
**You import the below Transport table into your model and have been instructed to find the totals across destination ZIP codes. Which summarization option would you recommend for aggregating the below three columns?**
**· DestinationZIP**
**· Weight**
**· Units**

| Table Name | Column Name | Data Type |
|---|---|---|
| Transport | ConsignmentID | Whole Number |
| | ShipDate | Date |
| | PickupID | Whole Number |
| | DestinationID | Whole Number |
| | DestinationZIP | Text |
| | Weight | Decimal |
| | Units | Whole Number |

A. MAX / NONE / SUM
B. COUNT / SUM / NONE
C. NONE / SUM / SUM
D. NONE / MAX / SUM

**Answer: C.**

Explanation
The answer is C.
The destination ZIP code is a text field, so do not use a summarization option. The weight is a decimal and we are interested in the total values, so use the SUM aggregation. Similarly, Units is a whole number and we are interested in the total values, so again use SUM.

**Question 40:**
**You work as a BI engineer at an Oil and Gas company. You are asked to calculate a year to date calculation on the sales across your dataset. You have generated a date table using M code that has the date and year field. You also have a calculated measure called 'Sales Total' which is the sum of the sales amount. See the exhibit below for the desired output in the column 'Sales YTD'. What are two ways to calculate the year to date sales from your data?**

| Year | Month Name | Sales Total | Sales YTD |
|------|-----------|------------|-----------|
| 2017 | Jul | $1,423,357.32 | $1,423,357.32 |
| 2017 | Aug | $2,057,902.45 | $3,481,259.78 |
| 2017 | Sep | $2,523,947.55 | $6,005,207.32 |
| 2017 | Oct | $561,681.48 | $6,566,888.80 |
| 2017 | Nov | $4,764,920.16 | $11,331,808.96 |
| 2017 | Dec | $596,746.56 | $11,928,555.52 |
| 2018 | Jan | $1,327,674.63 | $1,327,674.63 |
| 2018 | Feb | $3,936,463.31 | $5,264,137.93 |
| 2018 | Mar | $700,873.18 | $5,965,011.12 |
| 2018 | Apr | $1,519,275.24 | $7,484,286.36 |
| 2018 | May | $2,960,378.09 | $10,444,664.45 |
| **Total** | | **$109,809,274.20** | |

| | |
|----|----|
| A. | CALCULATE ([Sales Total],<br>FILTER(<br>  ALL(Date'),<br>  'Date' [Year] = MAX('Date' [Yea r]) &&<br>  'Date'[Date]< = MAX('Date'[Date])<br>  )<br>) |
| B. | TOTALQTD([Sales Total],'Date'&[Date]) |
| C. | TOTALYTD([Sales Total],'Date'&[Date]) |
| D. | CALCULATE ([Sales Total],<br>FILTER(<br>'Date',<br>'Date [Year] = MAX( Dat&[Year]) &&<br>'Date' [Date]< = MAXÇDate[Date])<br>  )<br>) |

**Answer: A, C.**

Explanation
The answer is A and C.
Answer A is the manual way to calculate the TOTALYTD function. In the filter, you first clear the filter context on the Date table using the ALL() function. If you forget to clear the filter context with ALL(), the aggregation will not work and will give the same value as the sales total for the month. The first part of the filter 'Date'[Year]=MAX('Date'[Year]) , ensures the year to date is limited to a single year and not the entire data set. The '&&' adds an 'AND' logical operator, enabling an extra filter expression. The second expression in the filter 'Date'[Date]<=MAX('Date'[Date]), ensures each time period is aggregated. The expression

134

ensures the aggregation is on or before the period in the table. Without the second expression, you would get the year total for each period.

Answer B is the total quarter to date. Since we want a year to date we need the TOTALYTD function not the TOTALQTD.

Answer C correctly gives the total year to date using the DAX function TOTALYTD.

Answer D is missing the ALL('Date') function to clear the filter context.

**Question 41:**

**Your manager at a construction materials company wants to know how category sales have changed over time with an animation. You decide that a chart with an animation to show changes across months would help visualize the data. How would you go about achieving this objective?**

    A.  Create a line chart and add month to the axis well

    B.  Create a waterfall chart and add month to the breakdown well

    C.  Create a scatter chart and add month to the play axis well

    D.  Create a tree map and add month to the details well

**Answer: C.**

Explanation

The answer is C.

The play axis is a feature on a scatter chart that animates changes with time. Create your scatter chart and then in the play axis well, add your date period. Below the chart you will now see a play button and a time axis.

You should not use a line chart with month in the axis well, as this does not animate the time series.

You should not use a waterfall chart as this is not the appropriate chart for a time series animation. Waterfall charts are useful for understanding how an initial value, such as sales, is affected by a series of positive and negative changes.

You should not use a tree map for time series animation. Treemaps are used to display hierarchical data as a set of nested rectangles.

**Question 42:**

**You are asked to create a measure to calculate the sales amount including the value added tax with the ability to go to the lowest level of detail (row level.) In addition, the value added tax is only relevant for order dates after Jan/1/2018. Prior to 2018, there is no tax applicable. See the exhibit below as an example of the output. How would you achieve this goal using a DAX expression?**

| Year | Month Name | Sales Amount | Sales Tax | Conditional Sales With Tax |
|------|-----------|-------------|-----------|---------------------------|
| 2017 | Jul | $1,423,357.32 | $142,335.73 | $1,423,357.32 |
| 2017 | Aug | $2,057,902.45 | $205,790.25 | $2,057,902.45 |
| 2017 | Sep | $2,523,947.55 | $252,394.76 | $2,523,947.55 |
| 2017 | Oct | $561,681.48 | $56,168.15 | $561,681.48 |
| 2017 | Nov | $4,764,920.16 | $476,492.03 | $4,764,920.16 |
| 2017 | Dec | $596,746.56 | $59,674.66 | $596,746.56 |
| 2018 | Jan | $1,327,674.63 | $132,767.47 | $1,460,442.10 |
| 2018 | Feb | $3,936,463.31 | $393,646.34 | $4,330,109.65 |
| 2018 | Mar | $700,873.18 | $70,087.32 | $770,960.50 |
| 2018 | Apr | $1,519,275.24 | $151,927.53 | $1,671,202.77 |
| 2018 | May | $2,960,378.09 | $296,037.82 | $3,256,415.91 |
| 2018 | Jun | $1,487,671.19 | $148,767.13 | $1,636,438.33 |
| 2018 | Jul | $2,939,691.00 | $293,969.12 | $3,233,660.11 |
| 2018 | Aug | $3,964,801.20 | $396,480.14 | $4,361,281.35 |
| 2018 | Sep | $3,287,605.93 | $328,760.61 | $3,616,366.54 |
| **Total** | | **$109,809,274.20** | **$10,980,927.69** | **$119,597,346.32** |

A. SUM(sales[Sales Amount]) + SUM(sales[Sales Tax])
B. SUMX(sales,if(sales[OrderDate]> = DATE(2018,1,1 ),sales[Sales Amount]+sales[Sales Tax],sales[Sales Amount]))
C. SUMX(filter(sales,sales[OrderDate] > =DATE(2018,1,1)),sales[Sales Amount]+sales[Sales Tax])
D. SUM(sales,if(sales[OrderDate]> ='1/1/2018',sales[Sales Amount] +sales[Sales Tax],sales[Sales Amount]))

**Answer: B.**

Explanation
The answer is B.
As we want to be able to calculate at the row level, we use SUMX. Within the SUMX expression, we can add an IF statement to test whether the date is after Jan/1/2018. If the statement is true then add the sales tax, otherwise, show the sales amount.
Answer A is not correct as it does not have a conditional statement for the order date.
Answer C is not correct, because it only shows values after 2018. Before 2018, the measure returns 0.

**Question 43:**
**At your company, you are the Power BI administrator. Your company policy states that only DA-100 certified people are allowed to create new workspaces. The people who are DA-100 certified are grouped into a security group called DA100Workspace. You hire several new people who have recently completed their DA-100 certification and assign them to the DA100Workspace security group.**
**The new users complain that they cannot create new workspaces. What three actions do you need to take in sequence in the admin portal to fix this issue?**

**Possible actions:**
  VI.    Navigate to Power BI admin portal and select Tenant settings
  VII.   Navigate to office 365 admin security and select settings
  VIII.  Choose specific security groups to apply to and add DA100Workspace
  IX.    Click on Workspace settings and then click on create workspaces
  X.     Click refresh

  A.  i / iv / iii
  B.  ii / iii / v
  C.  ii / iv / v
  D.  i / ii / iii

**Answer: A.**

Explanation
The Answer is A.
The steps to fix the issue in the Power BI admin portal are:
  1.  Navigate to Power BI admin portal and select Tenant settings
  2.  Click on Workspace settings and then click on create workspaces
  3.  Choose specific security groups to apply to and add DA100Workspace
You should not use office 365 security to change the workspace settings, these must be done in the Power BI admin portal. There is no refresh button you need to click to apply changes. After you have completed the three steps, you can click on the 'apply' button.

**Question 44:**
**You have built a dashboard for the board of a soft drink company. One of the board members has some ideas he wants to test with several visuals from a report page. However, he wants to be able to immediately see the updates in the dashboard after you make changes. How would you go about doing this in the most efficient manner?**
  A.  Create a new dashboard for every new request and pin the new tiles
  B.  Pin the report page as live to the dashboard
  C.  On the report page, select embed in dashboard
  D.  Create a hyperlink for the tiles and select embed in dashboard

**Answer: B.**

Explanation
The answer is B. Pin the report page as live to a dashboard. Any changes you make to the visualizations in the report editor, like adding a filter or changing the fields used in the chart, are reflected immediately in the dashboard tile as well.
You should not create a new dashboard every time a request is made as this takes time and is highly inefficient. On the report page, there is no select embed in the dashboard. There is no embed hyperlink in the dashboard option.

**Question 45:**

**You work for a rapid fashion company and are tasked with calculating the percentage change in sales from last month. You are given a measure Sales Total that aggregates sales and you have a date table you built in DAX. How would you calculate last month's sales percentage change?**

| | |
|---|---|
| A. | VAR SalesLastMonth = CALCULATE([Sales Total],DATEADDCDat& [Date], -1, MONTH))<br>VAR SalesPercentageChange = DIVIDE([Sales Total]-SalesLastMonth,SalesLastMonth)<br>Return SalesPercentageChange |
| B. | VAR SalesLastMonth = CALCULATE9[Sales Total], PARALLELPERIOD ('Date'[Date],=1,QUARTER))<br>VAR SalesPercentageChange = DIVIDE([Sales Total]-SalesLastMonth,SalesLastMonth)<br>Return SalesPercentageChange |
| C. | VAR SalesLastMonth = CALCULATE([Sales Total], SAMEPERIODLASTYEAR (Date[Date]))<br>VAR SalesPercentageChange = DIVIDE([Sales Total]-SalesLastMonth,SalesLastMonth)<br>Return SalesPercentageChange |
| D. | VAR SalesLastMonth = CALCULATE([Sales Total], DATEADD('Date'[Date],-1,MONTH))<br>VAR SalesPercentageChange = Sales Total-SalesLastMonth<br>Return SalesPercentageChange |

**Answer: A.**

Explanation
The answer is A. You can use DATEADD to look 1 month backward using the notation DATEADD('Date'[Date],-1,MONTH), noticing that the -1 indicates backward looking. Using the DIVIDE function, you can calculate the difference between last month and the current month's value and divide by the previous month to get a % change.
Answer B is not correct as PARALLELPERIOD uses Quarter instead of Month.
Answer C is not correct, because SAMPERIODLASTYEAR looks at the previous year's value and not last month's value.
Answer D is not correct, because the SalesPercentageChange does not divide by the previous month's value to get a percentage.

**Question 46:**
**Senior management wants you to add data classifications to your dashboards to raise awareness with those viewing your dashboards about what level of security should be used. For each of the following statements, select Yes if the statement is true. Otherwise, select No.**

| Statement | Yes | No |
|---|---|---|
| If data classification is turned on, all dashboards start out with a default classification type. | | |
| If you turn data classification off, all of the tags are remembered. | | |
| Each classification has a name, a shorthand tag and an optional URL. | | |

A. Yes / Yes / Yes
B. No / Yes / No
C. No / No / Yes
D. Yes / No / Yes

**Answer: D.**

Explanation
The answer is D.
When data classification is turned on in the tenant settings, all dashboards are given a default classification type. If you turn off data classification, none of the tags are remembered if you decided to switch on data classifications later. Lastly, each classification has a name and a shorthand tag. You can optionally add a URL with more information about your organization's classification guidelines and usage requirements.

**Question 47:**
**You have created a measure for the percentage of sales subcategory to sales and wish to apply conditional formatting as per the below exhibit. The rule you want to use is if the value is less than 10%, then shade the cell blue and if the value is greater than 10%, then shade the cell green. How would you complete the below conditional formatting table?**

| Category | Sales Total | Sales % Category |
|---|---|---|
| ⊟ Accessories | $1,272,057.89 | 100.0% |
|   Helmets | $484,048.53 | 38.1% |
|   Tires and Tubes | $246,454.53 | 19.4% |
|   Bike Racks | $237,096.16 | 18.6% |
|   Hydration Packs | $105,826.42 | 8.3% |
|   Bottles and Cages | $64,274.79 | 5.1% |
|   Fenders | $46,619.58 | 3.7% |
|   Bike Stands | $39,591.00 | 3.1% |
|   Cleaners | $18,406.97 | 1.4% |
|   Locks | $16,225.22 | 1.3% |
|   Pumps | $13,514.69 | 1.1% |
| ⊞ Bikes | $94,620,526.21 | 100.0% |
| ⊞ Clothing | $2,117,613.45 | 100.0% |
| ⊞ Components | $11,799,076.66 | 100.0% |
| Total | $109,809,274.20 | 100.0% |

Background color - *Sales % Category*

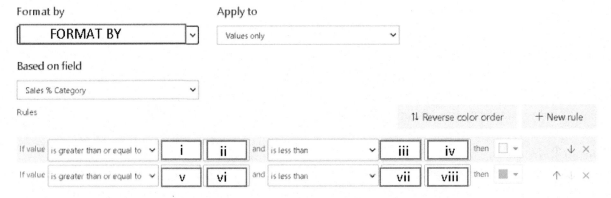

A. Format: 'Color Scale', Row 1: '0/ Number' and '10 / Number', Row 2: '10 / Number' and '100/ Number'

B. Format: 'Field Value', Row 1: '0/ Percentage' and '10/ Percentage', Row 2: '10 / Percentage' and '100 / Percentage'

C. Format: 'Rules', Row 1: '0/ Number' and '0.1 / Number', Row 2: '0.1 / Number' and '1 / Number

D. Format: 'Color Scale, Row 1: '0 / Percentage' and '10 / Percentage', Row 2: '10 / Percentage' and '100/ Percentage'

**Answer: C.**

Explanation
The answer is C.
When you have a set of specific requirements for your conditional formatting, select the rules format drop down. Next we know we want the first row to be greater than the number 0 and less

than the number 0.1, since 0.1 is the number equivalent to 10%. On the second line we want the color green for when we have a value greater than a number of 0.1 but less than 1.

You should not select a color scale as you can only set a minimum and maximum across the entire range. Here we have a specific set of rules we want to apply.

You should not use a field value. You can use field value when you have a separate column with the names of the colors you want to use.

Note, if you use percent instead of number for fields containing percentages, you may get unexpected results. The percent in conditional formatting gives the percentage of the given range. For example, our range for the accessories categories is 1.1% to 38.1%.

**Question 48:**

**You work for a winemaker who has a selection of white and red wines that are fermented in barrels. The process can take between 5 and 35 months. Your data set has columns for fermentation time, start and end date. You need to create a bar chart that shows wine fermentation time in ranges of 5 months. When creating the bar chart, which four actions should you perform in sequence?**

   A. Select the fermentation time column, right click and select New Group -> Set Group type to Bin -> Set the Bin type to number of bins -> Make the bin count 6
   B. Set Group type to list -> Select the fermentation time column, right click and select New Group -> Set the Bin type to number of bins -> Make the bin count 30
   C. Select the fermentation time column, right click and select New Group -> Set the Bin type to count of bins -> Set Group type to Bin -> Make the bin size 6
   D. Select the fermentation time column, right click and select New Group -> Set Group type to Bin -> Make the bin count 30 -> Set the Bin type to number of bins

**Answer: A.**

Explanation
The answer is A.
You should perform the below steps:
   1. Select the fermentation time column, right click and select New Group
   2. Set Group type to Bin
   3. Set the Bin type to number of bins
   4. Make the bin count 6
You should not set the bin count to 5. There are 30 months, each with a bin size of 5. This gives a bin count of 6. You should not set the bin size to 6 since the question specifically asks for ranges of 5 months, i.e. a bin size of 5.

**Question 49:**
**Your company has a current year target of last year's sales multiplied by an additional 10%. You have a date table called 'date' and you have a measure to sum sales called 'Sales Total.' How would you go about creating a DAX measure to calculate this?**

| | |
|---|---|
| A. | VAR PreviousYearSales = SUMX([Sales Total], SAMEPERIODLASTYEAR ('Date'[Date], -1, YEAR))<br>VAR TargetSales = PreviousYearSales*1.1<br>Return TargetSales |
| B. | VAR PreviousYearSales = CALCULATE([Sales Total], DATEADD('Date'[Date], -1,YEAR))<br>VAR TargetSales = PreviousYearSales*1.1<br>Return TargetSales |
| C. | VAR PreviousYearSales = CALCULATETABLE([Sales Total], DATEADD('Date'[Date], -1,YEAR))<br>VAR TargetSales = PreviousYearSales*1.1<br>Return TargetSales |
| D. | VAR PreviousYearSales = CALCULATE([Sales Total], PARALLELPERIOD ('Date'[Date], -1,MONTH))<br>VAR TargetSales = PreviousYearSales*1.1<br>Return PreviousYearSales |

**Answer: B.**

Explanation
The answer is B.
You should use CALCULATE and DATEADD to find last year's sales value. You then multiply the previous year's sales by 1.1 to get a 10% increase for the target.
In answer A you should not use SUMX as the first parameter is a table not a measure.
In answer C you should not use CALCULATETABLE as the result returned is a table and we want a scalar value. The CALCULATE function will return a scalar value. Also the target sales figure is multiplied by 1.1 and not 0.1.
In answer D, we want last year's value not last month. Also, the return statement should be for the target sales and not the previous year's sales.

**Question 50:**
**You work for a cryptocurrency exchange as a BI analyst. You are tasked with creating a report for weekly trends across the asset ranges. Your source dataset has over 150 million rows. What two things can you do to optimize the report performance?**
   A. Use the Direct Query storage mode for the dataset
   B. Only use line charts for visuals
   C. Use the Import storage mode for the dataset
   D. Do not use tab or layer order
   E. Create a summary table in the source data grouped by weekly volumes

**Answer: A, E.**

Explanation

The answer is A and E.

By using Direct Query for the storage mode, the data will not be held in the model. When a user views a visual, the queries will be sent to the database. However, performance of the query is dependent on the capacity of the data source. Additionally, creating a summary table that is grouped by week will reduce the model size. This will reduce the number of records that Power BI needs to process for calculations and visuals.

Limiting the model to only line charts does not affect the model performance.

You should not use the import storage mode. The import mode will bring all transactions into the model and give you an extremely large model. This will also mean the model will take a significant time to refresh the dataset.

Tab and layer orders do not affect the model performance.


**Question 51:**

**You work for a bicycle manufacturer and you have created a bar chart with sales by category. Your boss wants to know the median sales, the 50th percentile of values in a column, rather than the total sales for each category. What are the two ways to achieve this goal?**

    A.  Create a new measure using the MEDIAN DAX function on the sales column

    B.  In the analytics pane, add a trendline

    C.  In the chart values well, right click on sales and change the summarization to Median

    D.  Create a new measure using the Count (distinct) DAX function on the sales column

    E.  In the chart values well, right click on sales and change the show value as to a percent of grand total


**Answer: A, C.**


Explanation

The answers are A and C.

The first way is to create a DAX measure using the MEDIAN function. You could create a measure such as: Median of Sales = Median(sales[Sales Amount]). The other option is to right click sales in the values well and change the summarization type to Median.

You should not add a trendline. This will not help you find the median value.

You should not use Count (distinct) as we want the median not the count.

You should not use the percent of grand total as this will give you the percentage of all category sales.


**Question 52:**

**Your users give you feedback that they would like your reports to have more interactivity. You add some interactivity. To answer, select the following feature for each requirement from top to bottom. A feature may be used once, more than once, or not at all.**

**Features:**
- **Back button**
- **Tab selection**

- **Bookmarks**
- **Edit interactions**
- **Format pane**

| Requirement | Answer |
|---|---|
| Edit the way visuals within the same page respond when a data point is selected. | |
| Create a view of a report with specific filters applied. | |
| A way for users to return to the previous page. | |

A. Tab selection / Format pane / Back button
B. Edit interactions / Bookmarks / Back button
C. Edit interactions / Tab selection / Back button
D. Bookmarks / Edit interactions / Back button

**Answer: B.**

Explanation
The answer is B.
To edit the way visuals interact with each other on a report page use the 'Edit interactions' button after you select a visual. There are two options: cross-filter and cross-highlight. Cross-filter will filter other chars when you click on a data point. Alternatively, cross-highlight will highlight the proportion of the value when you click on a data point.
Bookmarks are used to store a report page and its configuration so that you can return to the view later. You can set the filters and slicers in a bookmark to get the visual configurations set in a certain way.
A back button has an arrow icon and when you select it, Power BI takes you back to the previous page.

**Question 53:**
**You find that your visuals on a report page are taking a long time to load and you need to find the cause. You remember there is a way to get how each of your report elements, such as visuals and DAX formulas, are performing. What five actions should you take in sequence from the below set of potential steps.**
- **Open performance analyzer and press start recording**
- **Ineract with the visuals**
- **Restart Power BI**

- **Press stop and review results**
- **Open query diagnostics and press start recording**
- **Click on SQL Server diagnostics**
- **Check enable diagnostics logging**
- **Create a blank report page**

A. Restart Power BI -> Open performance analyzer and press start recording -> Check enable diagnostics logging -> Press stop and review results
B. Create a blank report page -> Restart Power BI -> Click on SQL Server diagnostics-> Ineract with the visuals -> Press stop and review results
C. Create a blank report page -> Restart Power BI -> Open performance analyzer and press start recording -> Ineract with the visuals -> Press stop and review results
D. Restart Power BI -> Open query diagnostics and press start recording -> Ineract with the visuals -> Press stop and review results

**Answer: C.**

Explanation
The answer is C.
The steps to the performance analyzer tool are:
1. Create a blank report page
2. Restart Power BI
3. Open performance analyzer and press start recording
4. Interact with the visuals
5. Press stop and review results

In answer A, you should first create a blank report page and you do not need to enable diagnostic logging.
In answer B, you should not use SQL Server diagnostics, this is not available within Power BI.
In answer D, you should not use the query diagnostic tool. Query diagnostics is a Power Query tool to determine processing at authoring and at refresh time in Power BI Desktop. Query diagnostics does not tell you anything about visuals.

**Question 54:**
**You have a dataset in Power BI Service, and you want to use Quick Insights to get some ideas for a dashboard. However, you notice that Quick Insights are not working. What are the three possible reasons why Quick Insights is not working?**
A. You have uploaded data to Power BI
B. Your dataset uses Direct Query
C. Your dataset uses streaming
D. You have measures in your dataset
E. Your dataset is not statistically significant

**Answer: B, C, E.**

Explanation

The answer is B, C and E.

Quick Insights doesn't work with DirectQuery, streaming, and PUSH datasets. Quick Insights only works with data uploaded to Power BI. Furthermore, some datasets can't generate insights because the data is not statistically significant.

Uploaded data through import will work for Quick Insights.

Measures will work with quick insights.

**Question 55:**

**You have two visuals as per the below exhibit. You have the sales by year on the left, and on the right, you have sales by category. You need to configure the visual interaction between the two charts.**

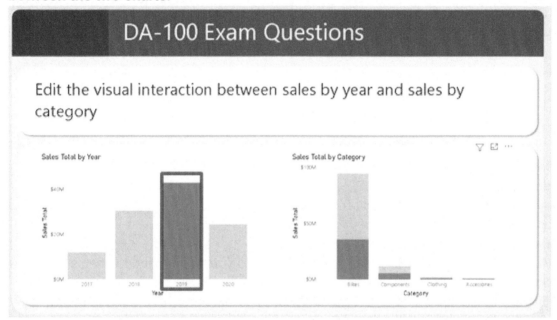

**For each of the following statements, select Yes if the statement is true. Otherwise, select No.**

| Statement | Yes | No |
|---|---|---|
| If you do not want the sales by year chart to filter the sales by category chart, set the interaction behaviour to None. | | |
| If you want the sales by year chart to highlight the sales by category chart, select the sales by category chart and edit the interaction on the sales by year chart. | | |
| To focus on the proportion of sales by category for a selected year, you should set the interaction behaviour to Filter. | | |

   A. Yes / No / Yes

B. Yes / No / No
C. No / No / Yes
D. Yes / Yes / No

**Answer: B.**

Explanation
The answer is B.
When you set the interaction behavior to None, the visual is not affected by other charts.
If you want the sales by year chart to highlight the sales by category chart, first select the sales by year chart and edit the interaction on the sales by category chart.
To show a proportion of sales by category when you select a year column, you should use the Highlight interaction behavior. The highlight will dim the non-relevant data so you can see the proportions as per the exhibit. If you use the Filter interaction, all non-relevant data is removed.

**Question 56:**
**Your company has a Power BI Premium license and you want to use the AI features in your report to expose insights. Which of the following two statements is NOT true?**
   A. You can take a piece of text and return a list of key phrases
   B. You can build your own machine learning models and use them in Power BI desktop
   C. The decomposition tree requires a premium subscription
   D. Sentiment Analysis is available for select languages
   E. You cannot use Power BI to tag images

**Answer: C, E.**

Explanation
The answer is C and E.
You can take a piece of text and return a list of key phrases using Key Phrase Extraction.
In Azure Machine Learning, you can create your own machine learning models. These models can then be used within the Power BI desktop. A decomposition tree is a standard AI visual and does not require a premium subscription. Sentiment Analysis, e.g. assigning positive or negative to a review, is available for select languages.

# Chapter 5: PL 300 Mock Test 3

**Question 1:**
**CASE 1**
**You have built a report with many pages for a manufacturing company. Your client's feedback is that it is hard to navigate to the important pages of the report. You suggest creating a homepage with links to help guide users to important pages on the report. How would you go about building the homepage?**
**Solution:**
- **Add pictures that describe the report page**
- **Set the image action type to 'Q&A.'**

**Can this technique be used for the homepage?**

    A. Yes
    B. No

**Question 2:**
**CASE 1**
**You have built a report with many pages for a manufacturing company. Your client's feedback is that it is hard to navigate to the important pages of the report. You suggest creating a homepage with links to help guide users to important pages on the report. How would you go about building the homepage?**
**Solution:**
- **Create a bookmark for each page**
- **On the homepage, create buttons to link to those pages**
- **On the button, change the action type to bookmark for the corresponding page**

**Can this technique be used for the homepage?**

    A. Yes
    B. No

**Question 3:**
**CASE 1**
**You have built a report with many pages for a manufacturing company. Your client's feedback is that it is hard to navigate to the important pages of the report. You suggest creating a homepage with links to help guide users to important pages on the report. How would you go about building the homepage?**
**Solution:**
- **Create shapes e.g. square, circle**
- **Assign the shape's action to page navigation**

**Can this technique be used for the homepage?**

A. Yes

B. No

## Question 4:

### CASE 2

You have a dataset for a market basket analysis as per the below exhibit. Each row represents a transaction, and each column contains an item purchased. For instance, in TransactionID 8 there are 3 products: Product1 = 'peanut butter', Product2 = frozen pizza' and Product3 =' ice cream'.

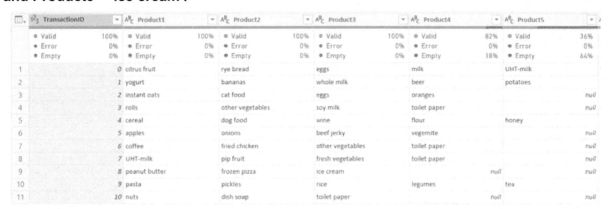

You need to transform your data into the below exhibit. The first column is TransactionID, the second is Attribute and the third column is Value. How would you transform the data into these 3 columns?

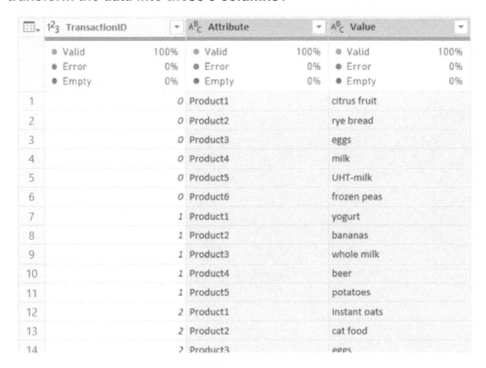

A. Select all columns -> Pivot columns

149

B.  Select TransactionID -> Select Pivot columns
C.  Select all columns -> Select Unpivot columns
D.  Select TransactionID -> Select Unpivot other columns


**Question 5:**
**CASE 2**
**For your Market Basket Analysis, you now need to create a new table with all possible combinations of products as per the below exhibit. What DAX function would you use in the [VALUE] position in the expression?**
**Basket Analysis =**
**FILTER(**
**[VALUE] (**
**VALUES('MarketBasket'[Value]),**
**SELECTCOLUMNS(VALUES(MarketBasket[Value]),"Value2", [Value])**
**),**
**[Value]>[Value2] )**

| Value | Value2 |
|---|---|
| rye bread | citrus fruit |
| eggs | citrus fruit |
| milk | citrus fruit |
| UHT-milk | citrus fruit |
| frozen peas | citrus fruit |
| yogurt | citrus fruit |
| whole milk | citrus fruit |
| potatoes | citrus fruit |
| instant oats | citrus fruit |
| oranges | citrus fruit |
| rolls | citrus fruit |

A.  INTERSECT
B.  EXCEPT
C.  SUMMARIZE
D.  CROSSJOIN


**Question 6:**
**CASE 2**

You want to use a custom network chart to display your market basket analysis called 'Network and add the Advanced Network Visual.' However, your company policy is to not allow custom visuals as a default. How could you enable this specific custom visual?

A. Temporarily allow all visuals
B. Add to organizational visuals
C. Reproduce the visual in R or Python
D. Place a request to Microsoft to add the custom visual to the standard charts

**Question 7:**
**CASE 3**
You are a Supply Chain analytics manager and have data on customer fill rates. A fill rate is a KPI of the fraction of customer demand that is met through immediate stock availability. See the below exhibit for a sample of the 'FillRate' table.
You need to restrict a visual to show the bottom 5 customers with the lowest fill rates.
Solution: Create a measure of the bottom five customers using the TOPN function.
Does this solution meet your goal?

| CustomerID | Fill Rate |
|---|---|
| 1 | 78% |
| 2 | 88% |
| 3 | 86% |
| 4 | 72% |
| 5 | 67% |
| 6 | 88% |
| 7 | 69% |
| 8 | 94% |
| 9 | 77% |
| 10 | 77% |

A. Yes
B. No.

**Question 8:**
**CASE 3**

You are a Supply Chain analytics manager and have data on customer fill rates. A fill rate is a KPI of the fraction of customer demand that is met through immediate stock availability. See the below exhibit for a sample of the 'FillRate' table. You need to restrict a visual to show the bottom 5 customers with the lowest fill rates.
Solution: Create a measure of the bottom five customers using the RANKX function.
Does this solution meet your goal?

| CustomerID | Fill Rate |
|------------|-----------|
| 1 | 78% |
| 2 | 88% |
| 3 | 86% |
| 4 | 72% |
| 5 | 67% |
| 6 | 88% |
| 7 | 69% |
| 8 | 94% |
| 9 | 77% |
| 10 | 77% |

A. Yes
B. No.


Question 9:
CASE 3
You are a Supply Chain analytics manager and have data on customer fill rates. A fill rate is a KPI of the fraction of customer demand that is met through immediate stock availability. See the below exhibit for a sample of the 'FillRate' table.
You need to restrict a visual to show the bottom 5 customers with the lowest fill rates.
Solution: Apply a Basic Filter on the visual (Visual level filter)
Does this solution meet your goal?

| CustomerID | Fill Rate |
|:---:|:---:|
| 1 | 78% |
| 2 | 88% |
| 3 | 86% |
| 4 | 72% |
| 5 | 67% |
| 6 | 88% |
| 7 | 69% |
| 8 | 94% |
| 9 | 77% |
| 10 | 77% |

A. Yes
B. No.

**Question 10:**
**You have created a dashboard you want to share with your suppliers to help with the data communications between your organizations. Your supplier has a Power BI Pro license and uses Power BI within their own organization as well. Prior to sharing your dashboard with your supplier, what do you first need to do?**
    A. Make sure your supplier has upgraded to Power BI Premium
    B. In the tenant settings, enable email notification service for outages or incidents
    C. In the tenant settings, enable share content with external users
    D. Publish your dashboard to the web

**Question 11:**
**You work for a software company that enables cryptocurrency payments for retailers. The key tables you have for your company's reporting requirements are:**
    1. **Date is a date table created in DAX**
    2. **Countries is a geographic table that is rarely updated**
    3. **Sales has the software sales to retailers and has many new records added every day**
**Which storage model should you use for each of the three requirements from top to bottom?**

A.   Import / Import / Live Connection
B.   Dual / Import / Live Connection
C.   Dual / Import / DirectQuery
D.   Import / Import / DirectQuery


**Question 12:**

**For your annual report, your company has produced a YouTube video. Your manager asks to add this YouTube video to your financial dashboard so the board members can see the video in the dashboard. How would you go about adding the YouTube video to your dashboard?**

A.   Add an image tile
B.   Add a video tile
C.   Add a text box tile
D.   Add a custom streaming data tile


**Question 13:**

**You have a large Power BI dashboard for stock prices that display weekly performance. The data set goes back to 1985. When the dashboard refreshes it takes too long to load. How would you optimize the model performance?**

A.   Add a personal gateway to your organization's dataset
B.   Add a streaming tile to your dashboard
C.   Adjust the time zone in the tenant setting
D.   Configure incremental refresh


**Question 14:**

**Your country has created a register for confirmed cases of COVID-19. The data is recorded in a large Azure SQL Database and is updated continuously. You have been contracted as a consultant to assist your government in creating a dashboard to visualize the data in Power BI. How would you configure your connection to the COVID-19 database?**

A.   Create a script to continuously import the data
B.   Connect to the data with Live Connection
C.   Connect to the data with DirectQuery
D.   Connect to the data with AI Insights


**Question 15:**

**You work for an electric engine manufacturer as a Power BI admin. You have two colleagues, Ray and Jane, who need access to your workspace. Ray will need to publish, unpublish, and change permissions for the apps. Jane needs to be able to publish**

reports to the workspace and delete content. What workspace roles should Ray and Jane be assigned?

- A. Ray = Member/Jane = Contributor
- B. Ray = Admin /Jane = Member
- C. Ray = Member/Jane = Viewer
- D. Ray = Member/Jane = Member

## Question 16:

Your company uses a transport provider that charges freight costs and fuel surcharge costs as per the below exhibit for the Transport table. How would you create a measure for the row-level average of the sum of freight and surcharge?

| ConsignmentID | Category | Freight ($) | Surcharge ($) |
|---------------|----------|-------------|---------------|
| 1 | A | 86 | 10 |
| 2 | A | 100 | 14 |
| 3 | B | 50 | 16 |
| 4 | B | 89 | 13 |
| 5 | C | 71 | 10 |
| 6 | A | 90 | 20 |
| 7 | C | 73 | 16 |
| 8 | A | 95 | 14 |
| 9 | C | 91 | 20 |
| 10 | B | 99 | 17 |

- A. AVERAGE (Transport, Transport[Freight ($)] + Transport[Surcharge ($)])
- B. SUMX(Transport, Transport[Freight ($)] + Transport[Surcharge ($)])
- C. AVERAGEA (Transport, Transport[Freight (S)])
- D. AVERAGEX (Transport, Transport[Freight (S)] + Transport[Surcharge (S)])

## Question 17:

You are checking your data for errors and want to see the average and standard deviation for a column. What data quality option should you use?

- A. Column quality
- B. Column distribution
- C. Column profile
- D. Monospaced

## Question 18:

You are the Power BI admin at your company. You have assigned a colleague as a member role in your workspace. What roles can she NOT perform?

- A. Update an app
- B. Manage dataset permissions

C. Update and delete the workspace

D. Allow others to reshare items

## Question 19:

You work in a warehouse for a large eCommerce company. You have a Power BI Premium dashboard of the key logistics metrics called daily shipments. You would like to receive a daily snapshot by email of the daily shipments dashboard. How can you achieve this goal?

A. Integrate the dashboard to Power BI Desktop

B. Ask the admin to add you as a contributor to the workspace

C. Subscribe to the dashboard

D. Turn on notifications on your instance of Power BI Service

## Question 20:

You are in Power Query Editor, and you see the below view across multiple columns. What data profile tool shows the image in the red box?

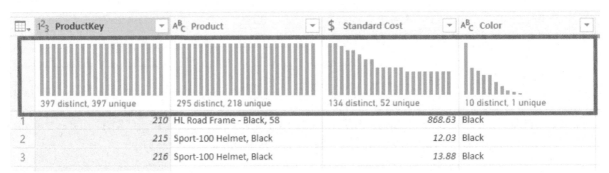

A. Column distribution

B. Column quality

C. Column histogram

D. Column profile

## Question 21:

You have two tables named Invoice and Geo that are connected through an active relationship using the GeoID field. You need to be able to filter the data from both the Geo table and from the Invoice table. I.e. you need the Invoice table filtered by Geo and the Geo table filtered by Invoice type. You have configured row-level security (RLS) so that Geographic leaders can only see the invoices from their region.

You are having difficulty getting RLS working for the relationship between the Geo and Invoices.

Which TWO actions should you perform to resolve this issue?

A. In the relationship view, set the cross filter direction to Single

B. In the relationship view, check apply security filter in both directions

C. In the relationship view, set the cross filter direction to Both

D. In the relationship view, uncheck make this relationship active

**Question 22:**

**You have four different data types and sizes. Select which file / files CAN be imported into Power BI Service without Premium capacity.**

| File type | File size |
|-----------|-----------|
| json | 200 MB |
| csv | 1.5 GB |
| txt | 500 MB |
| xlsx | 2.1 GB |

A. json - 200 MB

B. csv - 1.5 GB

C. txt - 500 MB

D. xlsx - 2.1GB

**Question 23:**

**Your company plans to use dataflows to process the data stored in the Common Data Service to prepare for Power BI reports and Dashboards. Where should you store the dataflows?**

A. Common Data Model folder

B. Azure Data Lake Gen2

C. Sharepoint

D. Azure SQL Server

**Question 24:**

**You are a Power BI User Admin. Which TWO tasks can you perform?**

A. Manage subscriptions

B. Create and manage users and groups

C. Enable and disable Power BI features

D. Reset user passwords

**Question 25:**

**You want to share a dashboard with external guest users from another business. How would you share content with external users?**

    A. Invite external guests through the Azure Active Directory B2B

    B. Click share directly from the dashboard

    C. Go to the Power BI admin tenant setting and add the emails for the external users

    D. Modify the workspace permissions to allow for the external users


**Question 26:**

**You think that a decomposition tree may be useful for your analysis. What TWO things does a decomposition tree do?**

    A. Conduct root cause analysis

    B. Segments that contribute to the selected metric value

    C. Visualize data across multiple dimensions

    D. Contrast the relative importance of factors


**Question 27:**

**You have an Inventory table and a Date table (see exhibit below) and need to calculate a semi-additive measure for the closing inventory value. How would you complete the below the [VALUE] field in the DAX expression?**

**Last Inventory Level =**
**CALCULATE (**
**SUM ( Inventory[Quantity] ),**
**[VALUE] ( [VALUE])**
**)**

| Table Name | Column Name |
|---|---|
| Inventory | TransactionID |
| | ProductID |
| | Category |
| | MovementDate |
| | Quantity |
| Date | Date |
| | Month |
| | Week |

    A. MAX / Date[Date]

    B. LASTDATE / Inventory[MovementDate]

158

C. LASTNONBLANK / Inventory[MovementDate]
D. LASTDATE / Date[Date]

## Question 28:

You work for a Bike company and create a report of Sales and Category. You build a measure for the Sales % of Categories and want to add conditional formatting such that the colors for low values are red, center values are orange and high values are green. How would you achieve this goal?

| Category | Sales Total | Sales % Category |
|---|---|---|
| ⊟ **Accessories** | **$1,272,057.89** | **100.0%** |
| Helmets | $484,048.53 | 38.1% |
| Tires and Tubes | $246,454.53 | 19.4% |
| Bike Racks | $237,096.16 | 18.6% |
| Hydration Packs | $105,826.42 | 8.3% |
| Bottles and Cages | $64,274.79 | 5.1% |
| Fenders | $46,619.58 | 3.7% |
| Bike Stands | $39,591.00 | 3.1% |
| Cleaners | $18,406.97 | 1.4% |
| Locks | $16,225.22 | 1.3% |
| Pumps | $13,514.69 | 1.1% |
| ⊞ **Bikes** | **$94,620,526.21** | **100.0%** |
| ⊞ **Clothing** | **$2,117,613.45** | **100.0%** |
| ⊞ **Components** | **$11,799,076.66** | **100.0%** |
| **Total** | **$109,809,274.20** | **100.0%** |

A. Use conditional formatting with a Color scale using default settings
B. Use conditional formatting with Rules
C. Use conditional formatting with a Color scale and check the diverging setting
D. Use conditional formatting with Field values

## Question 29:

You are working on a fast moving R&D project for an autonomous vehicle company. You create a dashboard but find that management wants you to make quick changes to both content and layout that they can see immediately on the dashboard. Management is only comfortable using a dashboard. What should you do to achieve this goal?
A. Create an app
B. Add management to the workspace as viewer roles

C. Create a refresh schedule for twice a day

D. Pin the report as a live page

## Question 30:

You have worked hard to create a clean dataset of all your company's customer details, including address and geocode. The Senior Director in your division has asked that all people within your company are aware of the high-quality, authoritative customer dataset that meets all the company's standards. How can you achieve this goal?

A. Select Promote content

B. Ask authorized reviewers to Certify your content

C. Select Featured content on home

D. Create a new workspace with the high-quality data and add the entire company as members

## Question 31:

You have a time series chart for your sales and you need to display a line to show the direction the data has moved over your selected period. How would you add this black dotted line? See the exhibit below.

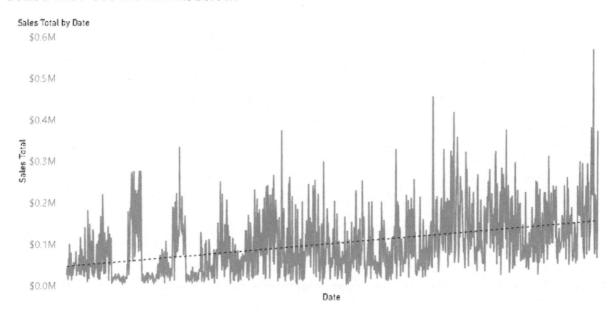

A. Add an Average line in the Analytics pane

B. Add a Trend line in the Analytics pane

C. Add a Forecast line in the Analytics pane

D. Add a Play Axis to the visual

## Question 32:

Your company is considering Power BI Report Server and you are asked if certain features are available. Which of the following three features are NOT available in Power BI Report Server?

A. Dashboards
B. Paginated reports
C. Q&A
D. Quick insights
E. Row-level security (RLS)

**Question 33:**

You work at a bike company and have two tables that use DirectQuery - Product and Category (see the below exhibit.) These two tables are joined with a relationship from Product to Category using the CategoryID column. To increase the efficiency in your join you decide to check 'Assume referential integrity' in the relationship. Will this help the join between your tables?

| ProductID | ProductName | CategoryID |
|-----------|-------------|------------|
| 1 | Mountain bike RX5 | 1 |
| 2 | Mountain bike 22L | null |
| 3 | Road bike S1 | 2 |
| 4 | Road bike P44 | |

| CategoryID | Category Name |
|------------|---------------|
| 1 | Mountain bike |
| 2 | Road bike |
| 3 | Bike clothing |
| 4 | Bike accessories |

A. Yes
B. No.

**Question 34:**

You are designing a data model and have a Date table and a Sales table as per the below exhibit. You create an active relationship between Date[Date] and Sales[Delivery Date]. You also create an inactive relationship between Date[Date] and Sales[Order Date].

161

How would you create a measure with the inactive Order Date by filling in the correct DAX function in [VALUE]?
CALCULATE (
[Sales Amount],
[VALUE] ( Sales[Delivery Date], 'Date'[Date] )
)

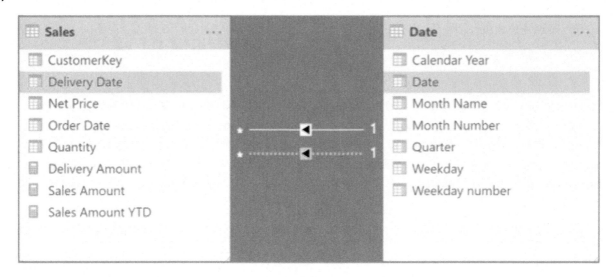

A. VALUES
B. SELECTCOLUMNS
C. RELATED
D. USERELATIONSHIP


**Question 35:**
**You are a Power BI consultant and you are doing some remote work for a mining company in Western Australia. You need to build a date table that starts from November 2010 and ends in December 2025. You decide you will use DAX to create a table. How should you create the DAX expression?**
   A. DATE (2010/11/1,2025/12/31)
   B. CALCULATE( CALENDAR('2010/11/1', '2025/12/31'))
   C. CALENDAR( DATE(2010,11,1), DATE(2025,12,31))
   D. CALENDAR( 2010/11/1, 2025/12/31)


**Question 36:**
**You import a TXT file that contains package delivery times. The format in the DeliveryDate column is in datetime format. For example, the first row is 2022-03-20 0831 EST. You want to analyze the dates, but you are not interested in the time stamp. How could you easily extract the date into a new column?**
   A. Use the TRIM function in a new column, then set the data type to Date
   B. Use the VALUE function in a new column, then set the data type to Date

162

C. Add a Column by example and type 2022-03-20, then set the data type to Date
D. Use the CONCATENATE function in a new column, then set the data type to Date


**Question 37:**

**You work for an established mobile App game company, and you have a large dataset for in-app purchases. The dataset contains over 300k rows. What visual should you use to identify outliers in the data?**
A. Key influencers
B. Decomposition tree
C. Scatter
D. Area


**Question 38:**

**One of your queries in Power Query Editor seems to be taking a lot longer to refresh than you expect. You need to understand what Power Query is doing at authoring and at refresh time. How would you go about this?**
A. Run Performance Analyzer
B. Run Q&A
C. Run Query Diagnostics
D. Run the ALM toolkit


**Question 39:**

**You have created a supplier quality report and are asked to add row-level security to your data model. You decide to add dynamic row-level security that uses a user's email address. You have a column for a user's email address called UserEmail. What DAX function would you use to create a new role using the UserEmail field?**
A. USEROBJECTID
B. USERPRINCIPALNAME
C. PATH
D. USERDOMAIN


**Question 40:**

**You work for a bank and have a large dataset for credit card transactions for a city. The data is in a Microsoft SQL Server database and has over 15 million rows. Before you use the dataset, you want to import a sample of the credit card data. How could you achieve this goal?**
A. Import all the data and then add a filter to the data
B. Add a WHERE clause to SQL statement in the advanced options
C. Change the data connectivity option to TOPN
D. Check HEAD to sample data from the advanced options

**Question 41:**

You have a slicer for categories in a vertical list. How can you get the same slicer into a horizontal list of buttons that automatically adapts to size changes, as per the below exhibit?

Category

☐ Accessories
☐ Bikes
☐ Clothing
☐ Components

Category

Accessories      Bikes      Clothing      Components

A. Add individual buttons and assign actions to each
B. Create several images and assign a bookmark
C. Change the orientation to Horizontal and toggle Responsive on
D. Change the orientation to Horizontal and change the background color

**Question 42:**

You have a customer service database that has a feedback score from 1 to 5. You create a dashboard with a card visual for the daily feedback score average. The CEO wants to receive an alert if the average score falls below 3.5. How can he achieve this?

A. Write a custom script in R
B. Create a subscription
C. Create a data alert
D. In the tenant settings, add an email for service notifications

**Question 43:**

You have a dashboard that is an important part of collaborative planning in your organization. Since the team is remote, you have been asked to allow users to provide feedback on the dashboard that will be visible to other team members. How would you achieve this goal?

A. Add sticky notes
B. Add comments
C. Add to group email
D. Add to alerts

**Question 44:**
You have an HR dataset divided into regions. You use row-level security to ensure each manager can only see their region's data. After you publish your report to Power BI Service, an HR manager calls and complains they cannot see all their data in the APAC region. How would you verify what the HR manager is seeing in Power BI Desktop?
    A. Validate the HR manager's role using 'View as' and select the region
    B. Use Track user activities
    C. Remove the HR manager from the role and re-assign
    D. Send the user your Power BI Desktop file


**Question 45:**
Your company has a Microsoft SharePoint site with all your manufacturing Bill of Materials (BOM) files in a subfolder. These files are all stored as Excel documents and have the same schema. As part of your analysis for the procurement team, you need to load all the Bill of Materials files together into a table in Power BI for analysis. You also need to edit some of the columns after the data has been loaded. How would you achieve this goal?
    A. From Get data, select SharePoint folder, enter the URL and click import
    B. From Get data, select SharePoint folder, enter the URL navigate to the specific folder and Combine & Transform Data
    C. From Get data, enter the URL select SharePoint folder and navigate to the specific folder
    D. From Get data, select SharePoint folder, navigate to the specific folder, select import or DirectQuery and specify any custom SQL code


**Question 46:**
You have a Date table with a date field called Date. You want to create a new column with the full month name and the year e.g. 03 October 2022. How would you create this DAX expression?
    A. FORMAT(Date[Date], "D M Y')
    B. FORMAT(Date[Date], "D MM YYYY")
    C. FORMAT(Date[Date], "DD MMM YYYY")
    D. FORMAT(Date[Date], "DD MMMM YYYY")


**Question 47:**
You have sales data for a bike company and you calculate a measure of the sales percentage within each category. You need to format the visualization to match the one shown in the exhibit.
How should you configure the visual?

| Category | Sales Total | Sales % Category ▼ | |
|---|---|---|---|
| ⊟ Accessories | $1,272,057.89 | | 100.0% |
| Helmets | $484,048.53 | ▓▓▓▓▓▓▓▓▓▓ | 38.1% |
| Tires and Tubes | $246,454.53 | ▓▓▓▓▓ | 19.4% |
| Bike Racks | $237,096.16 | ▓▓▓▓▓ | 18.6% |
| Hydration Packs | $105,826.42 | ▓▓ | 8.3% |
| Bottles and Cages | $64,274.79 | ▓ | 5.1% |
| Fenders | $46,619.58 | ▓ | 3.7% |
| Bike Stands | $39,591.00 | ▓ | 3.1% |
| Cleaners | $18,406.97 | | 1.4% |
| Locks | $16,225.22 | | 1.3% |
| Pumps | $13,514.69 | | 1.1% |
| ⊞ **Bikes** | $94,620,526.21 | | 100.0% |
| ⊞ **Clothing** | $2,117,613.45 | | 100.0% |
| ⊞ **Components** | $11,799,076.66 | | 100.0% |
| **Total** | $109,809,274.20 | | 100.0% |

A. In conditional formatting select 'Sales % Category' and turn on background color
B. In conditional formatting select 'Sales Total' and turn on data bars
C. In conditional formatting select 'Sales % Category' and turn on data bars
D. In conditional formatting select 'Sales Total' and turn on background color


**Question 48:**
**You work for an airline company and have a dataset with a DirectQuery storage mode. You have built a report with several visuals on the page. Users complain of performance issues when using the visuals in the Power BI report. How would you optimize the report?**

A. Under relationships, turn off security filters in both directions
B. Switch off single select under slicers
C. Switch off interactions between visuals
D. Remove any background images


**Question 49:**
**What data preview type would give you the below exhibit when you click on the Standard cost column?**

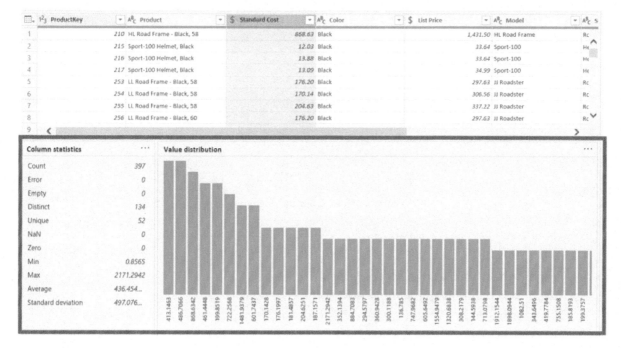

A. Column quality
B. Monospaced
C. Column distribution
D. Column profile


**Question 50:**
Your company is looking to expand your Power BI resources. Some of the feedback from your team is that it is hard to test Power BI Service dashboards fully prior to release. Is there a better way to handle the lifecycle of your Power BI report and dashboard creation? What is the best solution to achieve this goal?
A. Install Power BI Report server to test reports
B. Create a deployment pipeline across development test and production stages
C. Create separate workspaces for your team across the reporting lifecycle
D. Change to paginated reports for your reporting lifecycle


**Question 51:**
You have a product table, as per the below exhibit. You need to convert the Standard Cost column from a decimal number to currency. How would we achieve this using M code by replacing the below [VALUE] fields?
=Table.[VALUE] (#"Promoted Headers",{ {"ProductKey", Int64.Type}, {"Product", type text}, {"Standard Cost", [VALUE]} })

| 123 ProductKey | ABC Product | 1.2 Standard Cost |
|---|---|---|
| 1 | 210 HL Road Frame - Black, 58 | 868.6342 |
| 2 | 215 Sport-100 Helmet, Black | 12.0278 |
| 3 | 216 Sport-100 Helmet, Black | 13.8782 |
| 4 | 217 Sport-100 Helmet, Black | 13.0863 |
| 5 | 253 LL Road Frame - Black, 58 | 176.1997 |
| 6 | 254 LL Road Frame - Black, 58 | 170.1428 |
| 7 | 255 LL Road Frame - Black, 58 | 204.6251 |
| 8 | 256 LL Road Frame - Black, 60 | 176.1997 |

    A. TransformColumnNames / type decimal
    B. TransformColumnNames / type number
    C. TransformColumnTypes / Currency.Type
    D. TransformColumnTypes / type USE)


## Question 52:

**You work for a cryptocurrency exchange and have a report of crypto transactions showing monthly trends. Your crypto transaction table has over 60 million rows. You need to optimize the report's performance. Which TWO actions should you perform?**
    A. Set the storage mode on the crypto transaction table to Import
    B. Set the storage mode on the crypto transaction table to DirectQuery
    C. Create a summary table in the data source with the transactions grouped by month
    D. Limit visuals to bar and line charts


## Question 53:

**You work for a sports company, and you build a Power BI data set with row-level security in the data model. The company is divided into three categories: footwear, apparel and equipment. In Power BI desktop, you create roles for each category and you add a DAX filter expression for each role on the product table. You add the Azure Active Directory security group for the category to each role. A new user starts in the equipment category. What is the best practice to ensure that the new user can only view equipment data?**
    A. Add the user to the Azure Active Directory for the Equipment Category
    B. In Power BI Desktop, change the DAX filter for the role for the Equipment category
    C. In Power BI Service, add the new user's email address to the Equipment category
    D. Add the user's email to the workspace and change the role to a member

**Question 54:**

You lead a Power BI team for a turbine manufacturer. Your boss has asked your team to develop a custom 'pbiviz' visual in Power BI that shades the turbine areas according to the number of defects. Before you put together a team to develop the custom visual, you look into the steps to develop a custom visual to understand the skills required.

When setting up an environment for developing a Power BI visual, what software do you first need to install?

    A. C++

    B. node.js

    C. python

    D. R


**Question 55:**

You have recently set up a Power BI Service at your company. One of the senior managers expresses concern about publishing reports to the web with sensitive data. What can you do to prevent users from publishing content on the web?

    A. In the Admin portal, go to tenant settings and disable 'Allow content sharing with external users'

    B. In the Admin portal, go to tenant settings and disable 'Publish to web'.

    C. In the Admin portal, disable 'Allow URL links'

    D. In the Admin portal, enable 'Block embedded links'


**Question 56:**

You insert a product table into your data model and you find that there are two text issues.

    1. **In the product description field, you need to make ALL characters lowercase**

    2. **In the product model field, you need to remove trailing white spaces**

Which M code commands will help fix these issues?

    A. Text.Lower / Text.Clean

    B. Text.Proper / Text.Clean

    C. Text.Lower / Text.Trim

    D. Text.Proper / Text.Clean

# 5.1 Mock Test 3 Answer Sheet

**Question 1:**

**CASE 1**

**You have built a report with many pages for a manufacturing company. Your client's feedback is that it is hard to navigate to the important pages of the report. You suggest creating a homepage with links to help guide users to important pages on the report. How would you go about building the homepage?**

**Solution:**

- **Add pictures that describe the report page**
- **Set the image action type to 'Q&A.'**

**Can this technique be used for the homepage?**

A. Yes

B. No

**Answer: B.**

Explanation

The answer is B.

To use a picture as a link to a report page, the action type needs to be 'Page navigation'. If you select 'Q&A', the Q&A screen will pop-up to integrate your data.

**Question 2:**

**CASE 1**

**You have built a report with many pages for a manufacturing company. Your client's feedback is that it is hard to navigate to the important pages of the report. You suggest creating a homepage with links to help guide users to important pages on the report. How would you go about building the homepage?**

**Solution:**

- **Create a bookmark for each page**
- **On the homepage, create buttons to link to those pages**
- **On the button, change the action type to bookmark for the corresponding page**

**Can this technique be used for the homepage?**

A. Yes

B. No

**Answer: A.**

Explanation

This technique will work. A bookmark keeps a page in a configured format with filters applied. When you click on the homepage buttons, you are taken to the report page with the bookmark's settings applied.

## Question 3:
### CASE 1

You have built a report with many pages for a manufacturing company. Your client's feedback is that it is hard to navigate to the important pages of the report. You suggest creating a homepage with links to help guide users to important pages on the report. How would you go about building the homepage?

Solution:
- **Create shapes e.g. square, circle**
- **Assign the shape's action to page navigation**

**Can this technique be used for the homepage?**

A. Yes

B. No

**Answer: A.**

Explanation

The answer is A.

This technique will work. Page navigation is supported for buttons, images and shapes. When you click on the shape, you will navigate to the report page assigned to the shape.

## Question 4:
### CASE 2

You have a dataset for a market basket analysis as per the below exhibit. Each row represents a transaction, and each column contains an item purchased. For instance, in TransactionID 8 there are 3 products: Product1 = 'peanut butter', Product2 = frozen pizza' and Product3 =' ice cream'.

| | TransactionID | Product1 | Product2 | Product3 | Product4 | Product5 |
|---|---|---|---|---|---|---|
| | ● Valid 100% | ● Valid 100% | ● Valid 100% | ● Valid 100% | ● Valid 82% | ● Valid 36% |
| | ● Error 0% | ● Error 0% | ● Error 0% | ● Error 0% | ● Error 0% | ● Error 0% |
| | ● Empty 0% | ● Empty 0% | ● Empty 0% | ● Empty 0% | ● Empty 18% | ● Empty 64% |
| 1 | 0 | citrus fruit | rye bread | eggs | milk | UHT-milk |
| 2 | 1 | yogurt | bananas | whole milk | beer | potatoes |
| 3 | 2 | instant oats | cat food | eggs | oranges | null |
| 4 | 3 | rolls | other vegetables | soy milk | toilet paper | null |
| 5 | 4 | cereal | dog food | wine | flour | honey |
| 6 | 5 | apples | onions | beef jerky | vegemite | null |
| 7 | 6 | coffee | fried chicken | other vegetables | toilet paper | null |
| 8 | 7 | UHT-milk | pip fruit | fresh vegetables | toilet paper | null |
| 9 | 8 | peanut butter | frozen pizza | ice cream | null | null |
| 10 | 9 | pasta | pickles | rice | legumes | tea |
| 11 | 10 | nuts | dish soap | toilet paper | | null |

You need to transform your data into the below exhibit. The first column is TransactionID, the second is Attribute and the third column is Value. How would you transform the data into these 3 columns?

| 1²₃ TransactionID | | A<sup>B</sup>c Attribute | | A<sup>B</sup>c Value | |
|---|---|---|---|---|---|
| ● Valid | 100% | ● Valid | 100% | ● Valid | 100% |
| ● Error | 0% | ● Error | 0% | ● Error | 0% |
| ● Empty | 0% | ● Empty | 0% | ● Empty | 0% |
| 1 | 0 | Product1 | | citrus fruit | |
| 2 | 0 | Product2 | | rye bread | |
| 3 | 0 | Product3 | | eggs | |
| 4 | 0 | Product4 | | milk | |
| 5 | 0 | Product5 | | UHT-milk | |
| 6 | 0 | Product6 | | frozen peas | |
| 7 | 1 | Product1 | | yogurt | |
| 8 | 1 | Product2 | | bananas | |
| 9 | 1 | Product3 | | whole milk | |
| 10 | 1 | Product4 | | beer | |
| 11 | 1 | Product5 | | potatoes | |
| 12 | 2 | Product1 | | instant oats | |
| 13 | 2 | Product2 | | cat food | |
| 14 | 2 | Product3 | | eggs | |

A. Select all columns -> Pivot columns
B. Select TransactionID -> Select Pivot columns
C. Select all columns -> Select Unpivot columns
D. Select TransactionID -> Select Unpivot other columns

**Answer: D.**

Explanation
The answer is D.
To analyze the data you need as a minimum, a column for the TransactionID and a Value column for the item purchased. To do this, select the TransactionID column and then go to the transform ribbon and select Unpivot other columns.
Do not Pivot columns as per Answers A and B. Pivoting turns data into columns, whereas unpivoting turns data into rows. Since the exhibit shows data in rows, we want to use unpivot. Do not unpivot all columns as you will get two columns, attribute and value. The value column will mix both the TransactionID with the product purchased.

**Question 5:**
**CASE 2**
**For your Market Basket Analysis, you now need to create a new table with all possible combinations of products as per the below exhibit. What DAX function would you use in the [VALUE] position in the expression?**
**Basket Analysis =**
**FILTER(**
**[VALUE] (**

VALUES('MarketBasket'[Value]),
SELECTCOLUMNS(VALUES(MarketBasket[Value]),"Value2", [Value])
),
[Value]>[Value2] )

| Value | Value2 |
|---|---|
| rye bread | citrus fruit |
| eggs | citrus fruit |
| milk | citrus fruit |
| UHT-milk | citrus fruit |
| frozen peas | citrus fruit |
| yogurt | citrus fruit |
| whole milk | citrus fruit |
| potatoes | citrus fruit |
| instant oats | citrus fruit |
| oranges | citrus fruit |
| rolls | citrus fruit |

    A. INTERSECT
    B. EXCEPT
    C. SUMMARIZE
    D. CROSSJOIN

**Answer: D.**

Explanation
The answer is D.
You use a CROSSJOIN() function to combine each row from the first table with each row from the second table. For example, for every citrus fruit, there is a corresponding product. The filter function is used to remove duplicate rows.
Do not use INTERSECT(). The INTERSECT() function is used for the rows that exist in two tables.
Do not use EXCEPT(). The EXCEPT() function returns the rows of the left-side table which do not appear in the right-side table.
Do not use SUMMARIZE(), this function returns a summary of the input table grouped by specified columns.

**Question 6:**
**CASE 2**

You want to use a custom network chart to display your market basket analysis called 'Network and add the Advanced Network Visual.' However, your company policy is to not allow custom visuals as a default. How could you enable this specific custom visual?

A. Temporarily allow all visuals
B. Add to organizational visuals
C. Reproduce the visual in R or Python
D. Place a request to Microsoft to add the custom visual to the standard charts

**Answer: B.**

Explanation
The answer is B.
You can add custom visuals to your organizational visuals. Go to the admin portal in Power Bi Service and add the Network and add the Advanced Network Visual to your organizational visuals list. Now anyone in your company can use the custom visual.
Temporarily allowing all visuals would violate your company's policy.
Reproducing a visual is time-consuming and may not yield the same results as the custom visual. A request to Microsoft will unlikely add the custom visual to the standard charts.

**Question 7:**
**CASE 3**
**You are a Supply Chain analytics manager and have data on customer fill rates. A fill rate is a KPI of the fraction of customer demand that is met through immediate stock availability. See the below exhibit for a sample of the 'FillRate' table.**
**You need to restrict a visual to show the bottom 5 customers with the lowest fill rates.**
**Solution: Create a measure of the bottom five customers using the TOPN function.**
**Does this solution meet your goal?**

| CustomerID | Fill Rate |
|:---:|:---:|
| 1 | 78% |
| 2 | 88% |
| 3 | 86% |
| 4 | 72% |
| 5 | 67% |
| 6 | 88% |
| 7 | 69% |
| 8 | 94% |
| 9 | 77% |
| 10 | 77% |

A. Yes
B. No.

**Answer: A.**

Explanation
The answer is A.
You can use the TOPN DAX function to give the top or bottom values in a table. For instance, you could create a table of the bottom 5 values using TOPN and ASC such as the below.
Fill Rate Bottom 5 = TOPN (5, 'FillRate', 'FillRate'[Fill Rate], ASC)
If you wanted the same function to give you the top 5, you would change to DESC.
Fill Rate Top 5 = TOPN (5, 'FillRate', 'FillRate'[Fill Rate], DESC)
One thing to note is the TOPN function does not guarantee the order of the results. When you create your new table, you need to sort the Fill Rate column ascending or descending.

**Question 8:**
**CASE 3**
**You are a Supply Chain analytics manager and have data on customer fill rates. A fill rate is a KPI of the fraction of customer demand that is met through immediate stock availability. See the below exhibit for a sample of the 'FillRate' table. You need to restrict a visual to show the bottom 5 customers with the lowest fill rates.**
**Solution: Create a measure of the bottom five customers using the RANKX function.**
**Does this solution meet your goal?**

| CustomerID | Fill Rate |
|:---:|:---:|
| 1 | 78% |
| 2 | 88% |
| 3 | 86% |
| 4 | 72% |
| 5 | 67% |
| 6 | 88% |
| 7 | 69% |
| 8 | 94% |
| 9 | 77% |
| 10 | 77% |

A. Yes
B. No.

**Answer: A.**

Explanation
The answer is A.
You can use a RANKX function to rank your fill rates and then use CALCULATE and a FILTER to limit the output to the bottom or top values.

**Question 9:**
**CASE 3**
**You are a Supply Chain analytics manager and have data on customer fill rates. A fill rate is a KPI of the fraction of customer demand that is met through immediate stock availability. See the below exhibit for a sample of the 'FillRate' table.**
**You need to restrict a visual to show the bottom 5 customers with the lowest fill rates.**
**Solution: Apply a Basic Filter on the visual (Visual level filter)**
**Does this solution meet your goal?**

| CustomerID | Fill Rate |
|:---:|:---:|
| 1 | 78% |
| 2 | 88% |
| 3 | 86% |
| 4 | 72% |
| 5 | 67% |
| 6 | 88% |
| 7 | 69% |
| 8 | 94% |
| 9 | 77% |
| 10 | 77% |

 A. Yes
 B. No.

**Answer: B.**

Explanation
The answer is B.
A basic filter will not filter the bottom or top N items. However, if you use a Top N filter on the visual you can get the bottom 5 customers with the lowest fill rates.

**Question 10:**
**You have created a dashboard you want to share with your suppliers to help with the data communications between your organizations. Your supplier has a Power BI Pro license and uses Power BI within their own organization as well. Prior to sharing your dashboard with your supplier, what do you first need to do?**
 A. Make sure your supplier has upgraded to Power BI Premium
 B. In the tenant settings, enable email notification service for outages or incidents
 C. In the tenant settings, enable share content with external users
 D. Publish your dashboard to the web

**Answer: C.**

Explanation
The answer is C.

Users can share reports and dashboards with people outside your organization. The Share content with external users setting is found in the Export and sharing settings group.

Your supplier has Power BI Pro and does not need Power BI Premium to view your reports. Enabling email notifications for outages or incidents is not critical for sharing content outside your organization.

Publishing your dashboard to the web will make the report available for anyone on the internet to see. Since you only want to share the report with your supplier, this option is not appropriate.

**Question 11:**
**You work for a software company that enables cryptocurrency payments for retailers. The key tables you have for your company's reporting requirements are:**
4. **Date is a date table created in DAX**
5. **Countries is a geographic table that is rarely updated**
6. **Sales has the software sales to retailers and has many new records added every day**

**Which storage model should you use for each of the three requirements from top to bottom?**
   A. Import / Import / Live Connection
   B. Dual / Import / Live Connection
   C. Dual / Import / DirectQuery
   D. Import / Import / DirectQuery

**Answer: D.**

Explanation
The answer is D.

You should use the import mode for a calculated table and for the countries table. Since these tables will rarely change, import is the best option. The sales table should use DirectQuery as DirectQuery does not cache the data and is useful when using large amounts of data.

You should not use the dual storage mode. Tables with dual settings can act as either cached or not cached, depending on the context of the query that's submitted to the Power BI dataset. There is not a need for dual storage on this data set.

You should not use a Live Connection. A live connection is used for streaming data such as Analysis services from IoT devices.

**Question 12:**
**For your annual report, your company has produced a YouTube video. Your manager asks to add this YouTube video to your financial dashboard so the board members can see the video in the dashboard. How would you go about adding the YouTube video to your dashboard?**
   A. Add an image tile
   B. Add a video tile
   C. Add a text box tile
   D. Add a custom streaming data tile

**Answer: B.**

Explanation
The answer is B.
A video tile allows you to add a YouTube or Vimeo video to your dashboard, the video plays right on your dashboard. Do not use an image tile. An image tile is used for a static image such as a logo. Do not use a text box tile. A text box tile is used to add headings.
Do not add a custom streaming data tile. A streaming data tile is used for sensor data or feeds like Twitter.

**Question 13:**
**You have a large Power BI dashboard for stock prices that display weekly performance. The data set goes back to 1985. When the dashboard refreshes it takes too long to load. How would you optimize the model performance?**
   A. Add a personal gateway to your organization's dataset
   B. Add a streaming tile to your dashboard
   C. Adjust the time zone in the tenant setting
   D. Configure incremental refresh

**Answer: D.**

Explanation
The answer is D.
Incremental refresh allows you to refresh large datasets quickly and as often as you need, without having to reload historical data each time. Filter parameters for the start (RangeStart) and end date (RangeEnd) range are configured within Power BI Desktop. The incremental refresh policy can then be defined.
A personal gateway does not assist with the large data set.
A streaming tile is used for analysis service data and will not assist with this data set.
Changing the time zone in the tenant setting will not optimize the data performance.

**Question 14:**
**Your country has created a register for confirmed cases of COVID-19. The data is recorded in a large Azure SQL Database and is updated continuously. You have been contracted as a consultant to assist your government in creating a dashboard to visualize the data in Power BI. How would you configure your connection to the COVID-19 database?**
   A. Create a script to continuously import the data
   B. Connect to the data with Live Connection
   C. Connect to the data with DirectQuery
   D. Connect to the data with AI Insights

**Answer: C.**

Explanation
The answer is C.
DirectQuery is the best connection type for large datasets and no data is imported or copied into Power BI. Do not create a script to continuously import the data. To prevent the dataset from getting too large, use DirectQuery. Do not use AI Insights. AI Insights is a data visualization tool and not a data connection.

**Question 15:**

**You work for an electric engine manufacturer as a Power BI admin. You have two colleagues, Ray and Jane, who need access to your workspace. Ray will need to publish, unpublish, and change permissions for the apps. Jane needs to be able to publish reports to the workspace and delete content. What workspace roles should Ray and Jane be assigned?**

    A. Ray = Member/Jane = Contributor
    B. Ray = Admin /Jane = Member
    C. Ray = Member/Jane = Viewer
    D. Ray = Member/Jane = Member

**Answer: A.**

Explanation
The answer is A.
Ray should be assigned a member role. A member can publish, unpublish, and change permissions for the apps. Jane should be assigned a Contributor role. A contributor can publish reports to the workspace and delete content.

**Question 16:**

**Your company uses a transport provider that charges freight costs and fuel surcharge costs as per the below exhibit for the Transport table. How would you create a measure for the row-level average of the sum of freight and surcharge?**

| ConsignmentID | Category | Freight ($) | Surcharge ($) |
|---|---|---|---|
| 1 | A | 86 | 10 |
| 2 | A | 100 | 14 |
| 3 | B | 50 | 16 |
| 4 | B | 89 | 13 |
| 5 | C | 71 | 10 |
| 6 | A | 90 | 20 |
| 7 | C | 73 | 16 |
| 8 | A | 95 | 14 |
| 9 | C | 91 | 20 |
| 10 | B | 99 | 17 |

    A. AVERAGE (Transport, Transport[Freight ($)] + Transport[Surcharge ($)])

B.  SUMX(Transport, Transport[Freight ($)] + Transport[Surcharge ($)])

C.  AVERAGEA (Transport, Transport[Freight (S)])

D.  AVERAGEX (Transport, Transport[Freight (S)] + Transport[Surcharge (S)])

**Answer: D.**

Explanation

The answer is D.

The AVERAGEX function enables you to evaluate expressions for each row of a table, and then take the resulting set of values and calculate its arithmetic mean. We can calculate the sum of freight + surcharge and then calculate the average across all rows using AVERAGEX.

Do not use the AVERAGE function. AVERAGE() takes the average of a single column and does not allow for an expression at a row-level.

Do not use SUMX(). The SUMX() function would have to be combined with a COUNT function for the average.

Do not use the AVERAGEA function. AVERAGEA() takes a column and averages the numbers in it, but also handles non-numeric data types. The function does not allow for row-level expressions.

**Question 17:**

**You are checking your data for errors and want to see the average and standard deviation for a column. What data quality option should you use?**

A.  Column quality

B.  Column distribution

C.  Column profile

D.  Monospaced

**Answer: C.**

Explanation

The answer is C.

Column profile is a data quality option in Power BI that provides a more in-depth look at the data in a column. Column profile will give you a column distribution chart as well as key column statistics including average, standard deviation, min and max. Apart from the column distribution chart, it contains a column statistics chart that shows the average, standard deviation, minimum, maximum, and median values of the column, as well as the number of distinct values and errors. You can use column profile to see the summary statistics of a column and identify any outliers or anomalies in the data.

The other options are incorrect because:

• Column quality: This is a data quality option in Power BI that labels values in rows in five categories: Valid, Error, Empty, Unknown, and Unexpected error. Column quality does not show the average or standard deviation of a column, but rather the percentage and count of values that fall into each category.

- Column distribution: This is a data quality option in Power BI that provides a set of visuals underneath the names of the columns that showcase the frequency and distribution of the values in each of the columns. Column distribution does not show the average or standard deviation of a column, but rather the number and percentage of unique values and the most frequent values.
- Monospaced: This is not a data quality option in Power BI, but rather a type of font that has fixed-width characters. Monospaced fonts are often used for displaying code or tabular data, but they do not have any effect on the data quality or analysis in Power BI.

**Question 18:**

**You are the Power BI admin at your company. You have assigned a colleague as a member role in your workspace. What roles can she NOT perform?**

A. Update an app
B. Manage dataset permissions
C. Update and delete the workspace
D. Allow others to reshare items

**Answer: C.**

Explanation
The answer is C
A member can perform all tasks, except the 3 admin roles:
- Update and delete the workspace
- Add/remove people, including other admin
- Allow Contributors to update the app for the workspace

**Question 19:**

**You work in a warehouse for a large eCommerce company. You have a Power BI Premium dashboard of the key logistics metrics called daily shipments. You would like to receive a daily snapshot by email of the daily shipments dashboard. How can you achieve this goal?**

A. Integrate the dashboard to Power BI Desktop
B. Ask the admin to add you as a contributor to the workspace
C. Subscribe to the dashboard
D. Turn on notifications on your instance of Power BI Service

**Answer: C.**

Explanation
The answer is C.
When you subscribe to a dashboard and Power BI will email a snapshot to your inbox.
In answer A, you cannot integrate a dashboard to Power BI Desktop to receive a snapshot.
In answer B, being added to a workspace as a contributor allows you to edit and publish content but does not help receive a daily snapshot of the dashboard.

In answer C, notifications include updates to apps, alerts that have been triggered on dashboards, information about Power BI events and meetings, and new content added to workspaces. Notifications do not send snapshots to your email.

**Question 20:**

**You are in Power Query Editor, and you see the below view across multiple columns. What data profile tool shows the image in the red box?**

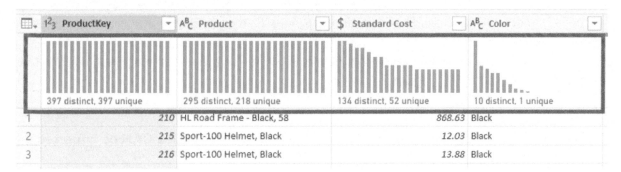

A. Column distribution
B. Column quality
C. Column histogram
D. Column profile

**Answer: A.**

Explanation
The answer is A.
The Column distribution shows a histogram of values and displays the number of distinct and unique items in a column.
Answer B is incorrect. Column quality shows the percentage of Valid, Error and Empty cells.
Answer C is incorrect. There is no option called Column histogram in Power Query Editor.
Answer D is incorrect. Column profile shows a distribution of a single column together with a number of key statistics.

**Question 21:**

**You have two tables named Invoice and Geo that are connected through an active relationship using the GeoID field. You need to be able to filter the data from both the Geo table and from the Invoice table. I.e. you need the Invoice table filtered by Geo and the Geo table filtered by Invoice type. You have configured row-level security (RLS) so that Geographic leaders can only see the invoices from their region.**
**You are having difficulty getting RLS working for the relationship between the Geo and Invoices.**
**Which TWO actions should you perform to resolve this issue?**
A. In the relationship view, set the cross filter direction to Single
B. In the relationship view, check apply security filter in both directions
C. In the relationship view, set the cross filter direction to Both

D. In the relationship view, uncheck make this relationship active

**Answer: B, C.**

Explanation
The answer is B and C.
To enable tables to be filtered in either direction, set the cross filter direction to Both. Also, to allow the security filter to work in both directions, check and apply a security filter in both directions. Do not set the cross filter direction to Single. Setting to Single will restrict the filtering in a single direction.
Do not uncheck and make this relationship active. If you make the relationship inactive, the two tables will not be able to join together.

**Question 22:**
**You have four different data types and sizes. Select which file / files CAN be imported into Power BI Service without Premium capacity.**

| File type | File size |
|-----------|-----------|
| json | 200 MB |
| csv | 1.5 GB |
| txt | 500 MB |
| xlsx | 2.1 GB |

A. json - 200 MB
B. csv - 1.5 GB
C. txt - 500 MB
D. xlsx - 2.1GB

**Answer: A, C.**

Explanation
The answer is A and C.
There is a 1-GB limit for datasets stored in shared capacities in the Power BI service. Only the json and txt files are under 1 GB.

**Question 23:**
**Your company plans to use dataflows to process the data stored in the Common Data Service to prepare for Power BI reports and Dashboards. Where should you store the dataflows?**
A. Common Data Model folder

B. Azure Data Lake Gen2
C. Sharepoint
D. Azure SQL Server

**Answer: B.**

Explanation
The answer is B.
You store your dataflows in Azure Data Lake Gen2. You can store the data from the dataflow using Common Data Model folders. However, you cannot store the data flow itself in a Common Data Model folder. You cannot use SharePoint or Azure SQL Server to store your dataflows.

**Question 24:**
**You are a Power BI User Admin. Which TWO tasks can you perform?**
    A. Manage subscriptions
    B. Create and manage users and groups
    C. Enable and disable Power BI features
    D. Reset user passwords

**Answer: B, D.**

Explanation
As a Power BI User Admin, you can perform the following two tasks:
• **Create and manage users and groups:** You can create and manage user accounts, assign roles and permissions, and control access to content and data in Power BI.
• **Reset user passwords:** You can reset user passwords for Power BI users in case they forget or lose their passwords.

The other options are incorrect because:
• Manage subscriptions: This is a task that can only be performed by a Billing Admin, who has access to billing and subscription management for Power BI.
• Enable and disable Power BI features: This is a task that can only be performed by a Power BI Admin, who has full access to Power BI management tasks and can configure the settings and policies for the Power BI service.
https://docs.microsoft.com/en-us/power-bi/admin/service-admin-administering-power-bi-in-your-organization

**Question 25:**
**You want to share a dashboard with external guest users from another business. How would you share content with external users?**
    A. Invite external guests through the Azure Active Directory B2B
    B. Click share directly from the dashboard
    C. Go to the Power BI admin tenant setting and add the emails for the external users
    D. Modify the workspace permissions to allow for the external users

**Answer: A.**

Explanation
The answer is A.
Power BI enables sharing content with external guest users through Azure Active Directory Business-to-business (Azure AD B2B). By default, external guests can only view reports and dashboards. Additionally, you can allow guest users outside your organization to edit and manage content within your organization.
- You cannot share a dashboard directly.
- You cannot add external user emails in the tenant setting.
- You cannot modify workspace permissions to allow for external users.

**Question 26:**
**You think that a decomposition tree may be useful for your analysis. What TWO things does a decomposition tree do?**
A. Conduct root cause analysis
B. Segments that contribute to the selected metric value
C. Visualize data across multiple dimensions
D. Contrast the relative importance of factors

**Answer: A, C.**

Explanation
The answer is A and C.
A decomposition tree is used to visualize data across multiple dimensions and can be used to conduct root cause analysis. A key influencer visual creates segments that contribute to a selected metric value and contrasts the relative importance of factors.

**Question 27:**
**You have an Inventory table and a Date table (see exhibit below) and need to calculate a semi-additive measure for the closing inventory value. How would you complete the below the [VALUE] field in the DAX expression?**
**Last Inventory Level =**
**CALCULATE (**
**SUM ( Inventory[Quantity] ),**
**[VALUE] ( [VALUE])**
**)**

| Table Name | Column Name |
|---|---|
| Inventory | TransactionID |
| | ProductID |
| | Category |
| | MovementDate |
| | Quantity |
| Date | Date |
| | Month |
| | Week |

A. MAX / Date[Date]
B. LASTDATE / Inventory[MovementDate]
C. LASTNONBLANK / Inventory[MovementDate]
D. LASTDATE / Date[Date]

**Answer: B.**

Explanation
The answer is B.
Use the LASTDATE function to get the last date of the Inventory[MovementDate] field. If you used the Date table with LASTDATE(Date[Date]), you may get a weekend or holiday when no inventory was recorded.
Do not use MAX or LASTDATE and the Date[Date ] field and you may get a weekend or holiday when no inventory was recorded.
Do not use LASTNONBLANK as this function expects a column and an expression.

**Question 28:**
**You work for a Bike company and create a report of Sales and Category. You build a measure for the Sales % of Categories and want to add conditional formatting such that the colors for low values are red, center values are orange and high values are green. How would you achieve this goal?**

| Category | Sales Total | Sales % Category ▼ |
|---|---|---|
| ⊟ **Accessories** | **$1,272,057.89** | **100.0%** |
| Helmets | $484,048.53 | 38.1% |
| Tires and Tubes | $246,454.53 | 19.4% |
| Bike Racks | $237,096.16 | 18.6% |
| Hydration Packs | $105,826.42 | 8.3% |
| Bottles and Cages | $64,274.79 | 5.1% |
| Fenders | $46,619.58 | 3.7% |
| Bike Stands | $39,591.00 | 3.1% |
| Cleaners | $18,406.97 | 1.4% |
| Locks | $16,225.22 | 1.3% |
| Pumps | $13,514.69 | 1.1% |
| ⊞ **Bikes** | **$94,620,526.21** | **100.0%** |
| ⊞ **Clothing** | **$2,117,613.45** | **100.0%** |
| ⊞ **Components** | **$11,799,076.66** | **100.0%** |
| **Total** | **$109,809,274.20** | **100.0%** |

A. Use conditional formatting with a Color scale using default settings
B. Use conditional formatting with Rules
C. Use conditional formatting with a Color scale and check the diverging setting
D. Use conditional formatting with Field values

**Answer: C.**

Explanation
The answer is C.
Use conditional formatting and under Format by selecting 'Color scale'. Next, select the 'diverging' setting and you will now have three color options: Minimum, Center and Maximum. Set the Minimum color to red, the Center color to orange and the Maximum to green.
Do not use a Color scale with default settings. This setting will give only two color settings, one color for Minimum and one color for Maximum.
Do not use the Format by 'Rules'. For rules-based conditional formatting, you will need a specific numeric range for each color and you will not be able to see a diverging color scheme as per the exhibit.
Do not use conditional formatting with field values. This conditional formatting setting relies on a column with color names or color codes.

**Question 29:**

You are working on a fast moving R&D project for an autonomous vehicle company. You create a dashboard but find that management wants you to make quick changes to both content and layout that they can see immediately on the dashboard. Management is only comfortable using a dashboard. What should you do to achieve this goal?

A. Create an app
B. Add management to the workspace as viewer roles
C. Create a refresh schedule for twice a day
D. Pin the report as a live page

**Answer: D.**

Explanation
The answer is D.
When you pin an entire page, the tiles are live. You can interact with the visuals directly on the dashboard. Changes you make to any of the visualizations back in the report editor, like adding a filter or changing the fields used in the chart, are reflected in the dashboard tile.
Do not create an app. Any layout changes will not be reflected in the app.
Do not add management to the workspace. This will not help them see an up to date dashboard. Note that they are only interested in accessing a dashboard and do not want to access the underlying workspace.
Do not add a refresh schedule as management wants to see updates immediately in the dashboard.

**Question 30:**
**You have worked hard to create a clean dataset of all your company's customer details, including address and geocode. The Senior Director in your division has asked that all people within your company are aware of the high-quality, authoritative customer dataset that meets all the company's standards. How can you achieve this goal?**

A. Select Promote content
B. Ask authorized reviewers to Certify your content
C. Select Featured content on home
D. Create a new workspace with the high-quality data and add the entire company as members

**Answer: B.**

Explanation
The answer is B.
Certification means that the content meets the company's quality standards and is regarded as reliable, authoritative, and ready for use across the organization. Only authorized reviewers (defined by the Power BI administrator) can certify content.
Do not select promote content. Promotion is a way to highlight content you think is valuable and worthwhile for others to use. It encourages the collaborative use and spread of content within an organization. Promotion is not used for authoritative, reliable data sources.

Do not select Feature content at home. When you feature dashboards, reports, and apps they appear in the Featured section of your colleagues' Power BI Home page.

Do not create a new workspace and add every person as a member. This will give your entire company the ability to edit your dataset and reports within the workspace.

**Question 31:**

**You have a time series chart for your sales and you need to display a line to show the direction the data has moved over your selected period. How would you add this black dotted line? See the exhibit below.**

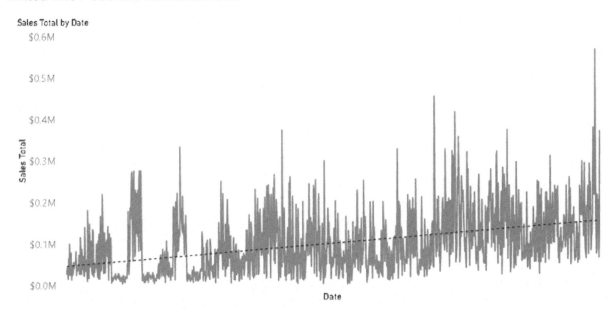

A. Add an Average line in the Analytics pane
B. Add a Trend line in the Analytics pane
C. Add a Forecast line in the Analytics pane
D. Add a Play Axis to the visual

**Answer: B.**

Explanation
The answer is B.
Power BI provides options to draw a trend line for visualizations using scatter plot charts and line charts. To add a Trend line, go to the Analytics pane and add a Trend line.
Do not add an average line as this will give a horizontal line that averages the data values.
Do not add a forecast line. A forecast line takes the historical data and estimates future values using a triple exponential smoothing algorithm.
Do not add a PlayAxis to the visual. A Play Axis is used to create an animation of a scatter chart across time.

**Question 32:**

Your company is considering Power BI Report Server and you are asked if certain features are available. Which of the following three features are NOT available in Power BI Report Server?

A. Dashboards
B. Paginated reports
C. Q&A
D. Quick insights
E. Row-level security (RLS)

**Answer: A, C, D.**

Explanation
The answer is A,C and D.
There are several features that are available in Power Bi Service but not available in Power BI Report Server. Of the listed items Dashboards, Q&A and Quick Insights are not available in Power BI Report Server. For a full comparison, see

https://docs.microsoft.com/en-us/power-bi/report-server/compare-report-server-service.

**Question 33:**
You work at a bike company and have two tables that use DirectQuery - Product and Category (see the below exhibit.) These two tables are joined with a relationship from Product to Category using the CategoryID column. To increase the efficiency in your join you decide to check 'Assume referential integrity' in the relationship. Will this help the join between your tables?

| ProductID | ProductName | CategoryID |
|---|---|---|
| 1 | Mountain bike RX5 | 1 |
| 2 | Mountain bike 22L | null |
| 3 | Road bike S1 | 2 |
| 4 | Road bike P44 | |

| CategoryID | Category Name |
|---|---|
| 1 | Mountain bike |
| 2 | Road bike |
| 3 | Bike clothing |
| 4 | Bike accessories |

A. Yes

B.  No.

**Answer: B.**

Explanation
The answer is B.
Assume Referential Integrity enables running more efficient queries against your DirectQuery data source. However, for referential integrity to work, data in the From column in the relationship can never be null or blank.

**Question 34:**
**You are designing a data model and have a Date table and a Sales table as per the below exhibit. You create an active relationship between Date[Date] and Sales[Delivery Date]. You also create an inactive relationship between Date[Date] and Sales[Order Date]. How would you create a measure with the inactive Order Date by filling in the correct DAX function in [VALUE]?**
**CALCULATE (**
**[Sales Amount],**
**[VALUE] ( Sales[Delivery Date], 'Date'[Date] )**
**)**

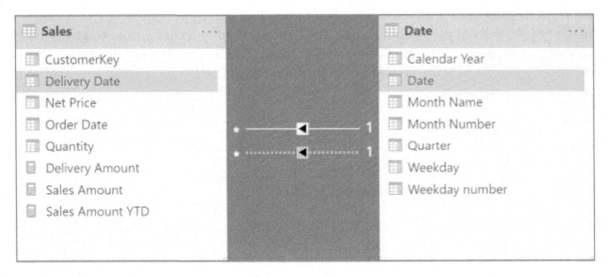

A.  VALUES
B.  SELECTCOLUMNS
C.  RELATED
D.  USERELATIONSHIP

**Answer: D.**

Explanation
The answer is D.

The USERELATIONSHIP function specifies an existing relationship to be used in the evaluation of a DAX expression. The relationship is defined by naming, as arguments, the two columns that serve as endpoints. As long as an active or inactive relationship exists, you can use USERELATIONSHIP in your calculation.

Do not use VALUES. The VALUES function returns a single column table of unique values.

Do not use SELECTCOLUMNS. The SELECTCOLUMNS function returns a table with selected columns.

Do not use RELATED. The RELATED function returns a related value from another table.

## Question 35:

**You are a Power BI consultant and you are doing some remote work for a mining company in Western Australia. You need to build a date table that starts from November 2010 and ends in December 2025. You decide you will use DAX to create a table. How should you create the DAX expression?**

    A. DATE (2010/11/1,2025/12/31)
    B. CALCULATE( CALENDAR('2010/11/1', '2025/12/31'))
    C. CALENDAR( DATE(2010,11,1), DATE(2025,12,31))
    D. CALENDAR( 2010/11/1, 2025/12/31)

**Answer: C.**

Explanation
The answer is C.
Use the CALENDAR function with a start and end date. For each date, use the DATE function and add in the three parameters for year, month and day.
In A, the DATE function is used to generate a single date and not a calendar.
In B, do not use CALCULATE and do not use strings within the CALENDAR function. Dates require the DATE function.
In D, do not use CALENDAR without the DATE function. The DATE function is required to convert the specified date in datetime format.

## Question 36:

**You import a TXT file that contains package delivery times. The format in the DeliveryDate column is in datetime format. For example, the first row is 2022-03-20 0831 EST. You want to analyze the dates, but you are not interested in the time stamp. How could you easily extract the date into a new column?**

    A. Use the TRIM function in a new column, then set the data type to Date
    B. Use the VALUE function in a new column, then set the data type to Date
    C. Add a Column by example and type 2022-03-20, then set the data type to Date
    D. Use the CONCATENATE function in a new column, then set the data type to Date

**Answer: C.**

Explanation

The answer is C.

In Power Query Editor, go to Add Column > Column from Examples. Next, and type in the date component of the first row you see e.g. 2022-03-20. After Power BI applies to all rows, set the data type of the column to Date.

Do not use the TRIM function. TRIM is used to remove whitespaces in strings.

Do not use the VALUE function. VALUE converts a string to a number.

Do not use the CONCATENATE function. CONCATENATE joins two strings together.

## Question 37:

**You work for an established mobile App game company, and you have a large dataset for in-app purchases. The dataset contains over 300k rows. What visual should you use to identify outliers in the data?**
   A. Key influencers
   B. Decomposition tree
   C. Scatter
   D. Area

**Answer: C.**

Explanation
The answer is C.

You should use a scatter cart to identify outliers in your data. Scatter charts are useful at displaying patterns in large datasets when displayed with two numeric values. You should not use a key influencer's visual. The key influencers visual allows you to discover factors that affect a metric. You should not use a decomposition tree. A decomposition tree allows you to drill into multiple dimensions and conduct root cause analysis.

You should not use an Area chart. An area chart (also known as layered area chart) is based on the line chart. The area between axis and line is filled with colors to indicate volume.

## Question 38:

**One of your queries in Power Query Editor seems to be taking a lot longer to refresh than you expect. You need to understand what Power Query is doing at authoring and at refresh time. How would you go about this?**
   A. Run Performance Analyzer
   B. Run Q&A
   C. Run Query Diagnostics
   D. Run the ALM toolkit

**Answer: C.**

Explanation
The answer is C.

The Query Diagnostics tells you what Power Query is doing at authoring and refresh time in Power BI Desktop. Performance analyzer is used to identify performance issues of visuals and is not used in Power Query Editor. Q&A is a natural language tool to help you interrogate your data and cannot be used to analyze queries. The ALM toolkit is a tool to manage Microsoft Power BI dataset and cannot be used to analyze queries.

## Question 39:
**You have created a supplier quality report and are asked to add row-level security to your data model. You decide to add dynamic row-level security that uses a user's email address. You have a column for a user's email address called UserEmail. What DAX function would you use to create a new role using the UserEmail field?**
   A. USEROBJECTID
   B. USERPRINCIPALNAME
   C. PATH
   D. USERDOMAIN

**Answer: B.**

Explanation
The answer is B.
Use the USERPRINCIPALNAME function. Within Power BI Desktop userprincipalname() will return a user in the format of user@companyABC.com.
In answer A, USEROBJECTID returns the current user's Object ID from Azure AD for Azure Analysis Server. This function does not return an email address.
In answer C, PATH returns a string that contains a delimited list of IDs, starting with the top/root of a hierarchy and ending with the specified ID. PATH is often used for employee hierarchies.
In answer D, there is no DAX function USERDOMAIN.

## Question 40:
**You work for a bank and have a large dataset for credit card transactions for a city. The data is in a Microsoft SQL Server database and has over 15 million rows. Before you use the dataset, you want to import a sample of the credit card data. How could you achieve this goal?**
   A. Import all the data and then add a filter to the data
   B. Add a WHERE clause to SQL statement in the advanced options
   C. Change the data connectivity option to TOPN
   D. Check HEAD to sample data from the advanced options

**Answer: B.**

Explanation
The answer is B.
When connecting to a SQL Server Database, expand the advanced options. Within the advanced options, you can add a SQL statement. Write a filter using the WHERE clause to import a sample of the data.

In answer A, if you import all the data, you will not have a small sample to work with. As there are 15 million rows, you may end up with a huge model that is difficult to use.

In answer C, there is no TOPN functionality. TOPN is a DAX filter used to create measures once the data has already been imported.

In answer D, there is no option HEAD in the advanced settings to automatically sample the data. HEAD is a function used in R scripts.

**Question 41:**

**You have a slicer for categories in a vertical list. How can you get the same slicer into a horizontal list of buttons that automatically adapts to size changes, as per the below exhibit?**

Category

[ ] Accessories
[ ] Bikes
[ ] Clothing
[ ] Components

Category

| Accessories | Bikes | Clothing | Components |

A. Add individual buttons and assign actions to each
B. Create several images and assign a bookmark
C. Change the orientation to Horizontal and toggle Responsive on
D. Change the orientation to Horizontal and change the background color

**Answer: C.**

Explanation
The answer is C.
Under the Format pane select the General dropdown. Under Orientation change the setting to Horizontal. Lastly, to ensure the visual will adapt to size changes, toggle the Responsive switch on.

In answers A and B, using buttons and images you cannot automatically adapt the size changes. These solutions also do not use a slicer.

In answer D, changing the background color does not assist with automatically adapting to size changes.

**Question 42:**

You have a customer service database that has a feedback score from 1 to 5. You create a dashboard with a card visual for the daily feedback score average. The CEO wants to receive an alert if the average score falls below 3.5. How can he achieve this?
- A. Write a custom script in R
- B. Create a subscription
- C. Create a data alert
- D. In the tenant settings, add an email for service notifications

**Answer: C.**

Explanation
The answer is C.
Alerts notify you when data in your dashboards changes beyond the limits you set. The limit can be above or below a threshold and can be set on cards, gauges and KPI visuals.
Answer A is incorrect. You do not write a custom R script for data alerts.
Answer B is incorrect. A subscription is a recurring snapshot of your dashboard sent to your email. A subscription is not used for data alerts.
Answer C is incorrect. You add emails for service notifications for admins in case of service disruptions.

**Question 43:**
**You have a dashboard that is an important part of collaborative planning in your organization. Since the team is remote, you have been asked to allow users to provide feedback on the dashboard that will be visible to other team members. How would you achieve this goal?**
- A. Add sticky notes
- B. Add comments
- C. Add to group email
- D. Add to alerts

**Answer: B.**

Explanation
The answer is B.
Comments can be added to an entire dashboard, to individual visuals on a dashboard and can be seen by your colleagues. Additionally, when you add a comment to a report, Power BI captures the current filter and slicer values and creates a bookmark. This means that when you select or respond to a comment, the report page or report visual may change to show you the active filter and slicer selections when the comment was first added.
- You cannot add sticky notes to a dashboard
- You cannot send a note to a group email through a dashboard.
- Lastly, you cannot add a note to an alert.

**Question 44:**

**You have an HR dataset divided into regions. You use row-level security to ensure each manager can only see their region's data. After you publish your report to Power BI Service, an HR manager calls and complains they cannot see all their data in the APAC region. How would you verify what the HR manager is seeing in Power BI Desktop?**

  A. Validate the HR manager's role using 'View as' and select the region
  B. Use Track user activities
  C. Remove the HR manager from the role and re-assign
  D. Send the user your Power BI Desktop file

**Answer: A.**

Explanation
The answer is A.
You can validate a role in Power BI Desktop by going to the Modeling tab and select View as. You can then check the APAC region to simulate what the HR manager sees. Do not use Track user activities as this will not show you what row-level security data your user will see. Do not remove the HR manager's role and re-assign. Only do this if you have established that the HR manager was incorrectly assigned to the wrong region. Do not send the user your Power Bi Desktop file as they will be able to see all region data, which they do not have access to.

**Question 45:**
**Your company has a Microsoft SharePoint site with all your manufacturing Bill of Materials (BOM) files in a subfolder. These files are all stored as Excel documents and have the same schema. As part of your analysis for the procurement team, you need to load all the Bill of Materials files together into a table in Power BI for analysis. You also need to edit some of the columns after the data has been loaded. How would you achieve this goal?**

  A. From Get data, select SharePoint folder, enter the URL and click import
  B. From Get data, select SharePoint folder, enter the URL navigate to the specific folder and Combine & Transform Data
  C. From Get data, enter the URL select SharePoint folder and navigate to the specific folder
  D. From Get data, select SharePoint folder, navigate to the specific folder, select import or DirectQuery and specify any custom SQL code

**Answer: B.**

Explanation
The answer is B. The steps to load a set of files from SharePoint with the same schema is:
  1. Get Data
  2. Select Sharepoint folder
  3. Enter the URL
  4. Navigate to the specific folder
  5. Select Combine & Transform Data

A is incorrect as you need to navigate first to the correct folder and there is no import button.

C is incorrect as you do not enter a URL prior to selecting the SharePoint folder as a data type.

D is incorrect as there is no custom SQL code. When connecting to Microsoft SQL Server, you can add custom SQL.

**Question 46:**

**You have a Date table with a date field called Date. You want to create a new column with the full month name and the year e.g. 03 October 2022. How would you create this DAX expression?**

    A. FORMAT(Date[Date], "D M Y')

    B. FORMAT(Date[Date], "D MM YYYY")

    C. FORMAT(Date[Date], "DD MMM YYYY")

    D. FORMAT(Date[Date], "DD MMMM YYYY")

**Answer: D.**

Explanation

The answer is D.

A "DD" will give a date field with a zero such as 03. A "MMMM" will give the full month name. The "YYYY" will give the full year.

Do not use A. The single "Y" gives the day of the year as a number. The single "D" and "M" give a single number for day of the month and month number.

Do not use B. The "MM" gives the month as a number e.g. 10.

Do not use C. The "MMM" gives the month as an abbreviation e.g. OCT.

https://docs.microsoft.com/en-us/dax/format-function-dax

**Question 47:**

**You have sales data for a bike company and you calculate a measure of the sales percentage within each category. You need to format the visualization to match the one shown in the exhibit.**

**How should you configure the visual?**

| Category | Sales Total | Sales % Category ▼ |
|---|---|---|
| ⊟ Accessories | $1,272,057.89 | 100.0% |
|    Helmets | $484,048.53 | 38.1% |
|    Tires and Tubes | $246,454.53 | 19.4% |
|    Bike Racks | $237,096.16 | 18.6% |
|    Hydration Packs | $105,826.42 | 8.3% |
|    Bottles and Cages | $64,274.79 | 5.1% |
|    Fenders | $46,619.58 | 3.7% |
|    Bike Stands | $39,591.00 | 3.1% |
|    Cleaners | $18,406.97 | 1.4% |
|    Locks | $16,225.22 | 1.3% |
|    Pumps | $13,514.69 | 1.1% |
| ⊞ Bikes | $94,620,526.21 | 100.0% |
| ⊞ Clothing | $2,117,613.45 | 100.0% |
| ⊞ Components | $11,799,076.66 | 100.0% |
| Total | $109,809,274.20 | 100.0% |

A. In conditional formatting select 'Sales % Category' and turn on background color
B. In conditional formatting select 'Sales Total' and turn on data bars
C. In conditional formatting select 'Sales % Category' and turn on data bars
D. In conditional formatting select 'Sales Total' and turn on background color

**Answer: C.**

Explanation
The answer is C.
In the format pane, expand conditional formatting. Select the column 'Sales % Category' from the dropdown and then turn on data bars.

**Question 48:**
**You work for an airline company and have a dataset with a DirectQuery storage mode. You have built a report with several visuals on the page. Users complain of performance issues when using the visuals in the Power BI report. How would you optimize the report?**
   A. Under relationships, turn off security filters in both directions
   B. Switch off single select under slicers
   C. Switch off interactions between visuals
   D. Remove any background images

**Answer: C.**

Explanation
The answer is C.

You should switch off interactions between visuals. Cross-filtering and cross-highlighting interactions cause queries to submit to the data source every time a user clicks on a visual when DirectQuery is used. You can disable interactions at the report level or for each visual on the page that is causing issues to fix the performance issue.

In answer A, turning off security filters will not optimize the report and may be necessary for row-level security.

In answer B, switching off single select for slicers will create more inefficiency. Single select is more optimal than multi-select.

In answer D, removing background images will have a negligible impact to report optimization.

## Question 49:

**What data preview type would give you the below exhibit when you click on the Standard cost column?**

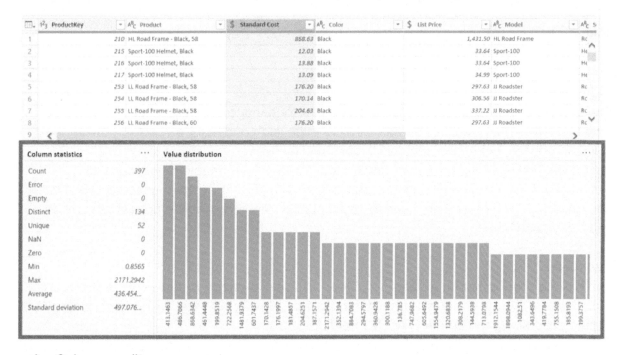

- A. Column quality
- B. Monospaced
- C. Column distribution
- D. Column profile

**Answer: D.**

Explanation
The answer is D.
The column profile feature provides a more in-depth look at the data in a column. Apart from the column distribution chart, it contains a column statistics chart.
Column quality shows the valid, error and empty percentages across all columns.
Monospaced applies a monospaced font to the data.

Column distribution provides a set of visuals underneath the names of the columns that showcase the frequency and distribution of the values in each of the columns. The data in these visualizations is sorted in descending order from the value with the highest frequency.

## Question 50:

**Your company is looking to expand your Power BI resources. Some of the feedback from your team is that it is hard to test Power BI Service dashboards fully prior to release. Is there a better way to handle the lifecycle of your Power BI report and dashboard creation? What is the best solution to achieve this goal?**
  A. Install Power BI Report server to test reports
  B. Create a deployment pipeline across development test and production stages
  C. Create separate workspaces for your team across the reporting lifecycle
  D. Change to paginated reports for your reporting lifecycle

**Answer: B.**

Explanation
The answer is B.
The deployment pipelines tool enables BI creators to manage the lifecycle of organizational content. Deployment pipelines enable creators to develop and test Power BI content in the Power BI service, before the content is consumed by users.
Do not use Power BI Report Server, as this tool alone will not enable report lifecycle management. Creating separate workspaces is not an efficient way to manage a deployment lifecycle. Paginated reports are used for 'pixel perfect' reporting and will not assist in report lifecycle management.

## Question 51:

**You have a product table, as per the below exhibit. You need to convert the Standard Cost column from a decimal number to currency. How would we achieve this using M code by replacing the below [VALUE] fields?**
**=Table.[VALUE] (#"Promoted Headers",{ {"ProductKey", Int64.Type}, {"Product", type text}, {"Standard Cost", [VALUE]} })**

| 123 ProductKey | ABC Product | 1.2 Standard Cost |
|---|---|---|
| 1 | 210 HL Road Frame - Black, 58 | 868.6342 |
| 2 | 215 Sport-100 Helmet, Black | 12.0278 |
| 3 | 216 Sport-100 Helmet, Black | 13.8782 |
| 4 | 217 Sport-100 Helmet, Black | 13.0863 |
| 5 | 253 LL Road Frame - Black, 58 | 176.1997 |

| | | | |
|---|---|---|---|
| 6 | 254 | LL Road Frame - Black, 58 | 170.1428 |
| 7 | 255 | LL Road Frame - Black, 58 | 204.6251 |
| 8 | 256 | LL Road Frame - Black, 60 | 176.1997 |

A. TransformColumnNames / type decimal
B. TransformColumnNames / type number
C. TransformColumnTypes / Currency.Type
D. TransformColumnTypes / type USE)

**Answer: C.**

Explanation
The answer is C.
Use Table. TransformColumnTypes to transform columns from one type to another. When converting from decimal to currency, use the Currency.Type parameter. Do not use TransformColumnNames as this changes the name of the column and not the data type. There is no type USD. Common data types are type number (decimal), Int64.Type (integer), type text (text) and Percentage.Type (percentage).

**Question 52:**
**You work for a cryptocurrency exchange and have a report of crypto transactions showing monthly trends. Your crypto transaction table has over 60 million rows. You need to optimize the report's performance. Which TWO actions should you perform?**
   A. Set the storage mode on the crypto transaction table to Import
   B. Set the storage mode on the crypto transaction table to DirectQuery
   C. Create a summary table in the data source with the transactions grouped by month
   D. Limit visuals to bar and line charts

**Answer: B, C.**

Explanation
The answer is B and C.
By creating a summary table at a monthly level, the amount of data that Power BI needs to process is significantly reduced. Furthermore, setting the storage mode on the crypto transaction table to DirectQuery means no data is imported or copied into Power BI Desktop. As you create or interact with a visualization, Power BI Desktop queries the underlying data source, so you are always viewing current data.
Do not import the crypto transaction table as the 60 million row data set will create a huge data model and you need the flexibility to query the most up to date data.
Limiting the visual types to bar and line charts will not have an impact on the data model.

**Question 53:**

You work for a sports company, and you build a Power BI data set with row-level security in the data model. The company is divided into three categories: footwear, apparel and equipment. In Power BI desktop, you create roles for each category and you add a DAX filter expression for each role on the product table. You add the Azure Active Directory security group for the category to each role. A new user starts in the equipment category. What is the best practice to ensure that the new user can only view equipment data?

A. Add the user to the Azure Active Directory for the Equipment Category
B. In Power BI Desktop, change the DAX filter for the role for the Equipment category
C. In Power BI Service, add the new user's email address to the Equipment category
D. Add the user's email to the workspace and change the role to a member

**Answer: A.**

Explanation
The answer is A.

The new user should be added to the Azure Active Directory for the Equipment category. Since you have used Azure Active Directory security groups to control membership of the roles, you should add and remove users using the Azure Active Directory.

Do not change the DAX filter in Power BI Desktop. The DAX expression is used as a filter on rows displayed for a role and does not control the membership of that role. Membership of roles can either be managed in Azure Active Directory or in Power BI Service.

While it is possible to add the user's email to a role in Power BI Service, it is not best practice in this case because you have already set up Azure Active Directory groups to control the membership of roles.

Adding the user as a workspace member does not assist in row-level security. In the Power BI Service, members of a workspace have access to datasets in the workspace. Row-level security does not restrict this data access.

**Question 54:**
You lead a Power BI team for a turbine manufacturer. Your boss has asked your team to develop a custom 'pbiviz' visual in Power BI that shades the turbine areas according to the number of defects. Before you put together a team to develop the custom visual, you look into the steps to develop a custom visual to understand the skills required.
When setting up an environment for developing a Power BI visual, what software do you first need to install?

A. C++
B. node.js
C. python
D. R

**Answer: B.**

Explanation

The answer is B. To develop **pbiviz** files, you need to install node.js, a framework designed to build scalable applications based on the Javascript language. The steps to set up an environment for a custom visual are:

1. Install nodes.js
2. Install pbiviz
3. Create and install a certificate
4. Set up Power BI service for developing a visual
5. Install additional libraries (required for developing a visual, e.g. D3)

Do not install c++, as this language cannot be used for pbiviz files. While python and R can be used to create custom visuals within Power BI, they cannot be used to create pbiviz files.

**Question 55:**

**You have recently set up a Power BI Service at your company. One of the senior managers expresses concern about publishing reports to the web with sensitive data. What can you do to prevent users from publishing content on the web?**

    A. In the Admin portal, go to tenant settings and disable 'Allow content sharing with external users'
    B. In the Admin portal, go to tenant settings and disable 'Publish to web'.
    C. In the Admin portal, disable 'Allow URL links'
    D. In the Admin portal, enable 'Block embedded links'

**Answer: B.**

Explanation
The answer is B.
To disable the ability for users to publish to the web, go to Admin Portal > Tenant settings > under Publish to web, check disable. This setting allows you to control whether users can use the publish to the web feature.
Do not disable Allow content sharing with external users. You may need this functionality to share reports and workspaces with approved external users. There are no settings 'Allow URL links' nor 'Block embedded links'.

**Question 56:**

**You insert a product table into your data model and you find that there are two text issues.**

    1. **In the product description field, you need to make ALL characters lowercase**
    2. **In the product model field, you need to remove trailing white spaces**

**Which M code commands will help fix these issues?**

    A. Text.Lower / Text.Clean
    B. Text.Proper / Text.Clean
    C. Text.Lower / Text.Trim
    D. Text.Proper / Text.Clean

**Answer: C.**

Explanation
The answer is C.
To transform all of the text to lowercase use Text.Lower. To remove leading or trailing whitespaces, use Text.Trim. Do not use Text.Clean, this function is used to remove non-printable characters such as line feeds and other control characters. Do not use Text.Proper, this function capitalizes the first letter in each word.

Dedicated for your Abound success

Notes…

Notes…

Notes…

Notes…

Printed in Great Britain
by Amazon

43915182R00117